Creative Approaches to Physical Education

Creative Approaches to Physical Education

Helping children to achieve their true potential

Edited by Jim Lavin

Routledge
Taylor & Francis Group

LONDON AND NEW YORK

First published 2008 by Routledge
2 Park Square, Milton Park, Abingdon, Oxon, OX14 4RN

Simultaneously published in the USA and Canada
by Routledge
270 Madison Avenue, New York, NY 10016

Routledge is an imprint of the Taylor & Francis Group

© 2008 Jim Lavin

Typeset in Garamond by Prepress Projects Ltd, Perth, UK
Printed and bound in Great Britain by TJ International, Padstow, Cornwall

British Library Cataloguing in Publication Data
A catalogue record for this book is available from the British Library

Library of Congress Cataloging-in-Publication Data
Creative approaches to physical education : helping children to achieve their true poten-
tial / edited by Jim Lavin.
    p. cm.
    Includes bibliographical references and index.
ISBN 978-0-415-44588-7 (pbk. : alk. paper) — ISBN 978-0-203-92784-7 (ebook)
1. Physical education for children—Study and teaching (Elementary)—Great Britain. 2.
Physical fitness for children—Study and teaching (Elementary)—Great Britain. I. Lavin,
Jim.
    GV443.C74 2008
    613.7'042—dc22
    2007044887

ISBN10: 0–415–44588–4 (pbk)
ISBN10: 0–203–92784–2 (ebk)
ISBN13: 978–0–415–44588–7 (pbk)
ISBN13: 978–0–203–92784–7 (ebk)

Contents

Illustrations

Figures

Boxes

Tables

Contributors

Alison Chapman is Senior Lecturer in Physical Education at the University of Cumbria. She has a breadth of experience working in secondary education in a range of roles including Head of Physical Education, Head of Year and, more recently, Assistant Head Teacher and Director of Sport in a specialist sports college. She also has experience in a number of different GCSE and A level courses and has a special interest in dance, having developed several dance departments in comprehensive schools.

Nigel Clarke is a senior lecturer in physical education at the University of Cumbria, where he has led the secondary PE programme. His teaching career began in East Yorkshire, where he taught secondary PE for twelve years before moving to teach in South Lakeland. His research interests lie in childhood obesity and the use of ICT in physical education.

Jo Harris is currently Director of the Teacher Education Unit in the School of Sport and Exercise Science, Loughborough University. Jo has a distinguished record of service to the physical education teaching profession. She was President of the Physical Education Association of the United Kingdom for three years (2003–06) and is currently on the management board of the Association for Physical Education. Jo regularly carries out external examining duties and presents at national and international conferences.

Jim Lavin is Principal Lecturer in Physical Education at the University of Cumbria where he leads the physical education teacher training courses. He has taught in both primary and secondary schools and was head of PE in a large comprehensive school before moving into higher education. His main research interests relate to creative and cooperative forms of physical education.

Richard Lemmey is Head of School of Outdoor Studies at the University of Cumbria. Initially working in fish farming and hill farming, Richard's love of the outdoors led him into youth work and then into teaching. When he moved to what was then Charlotte Mason College, he became involved in the evolution of courses that have led to the current outdoor degrees. His main professional interests are creative approaches to outdoor education, ecology and human perceptions of the outdoors. He is a keen sea-kayaker.

Lawry Price is Assistant Dean (Learning and Teaching) and Principal Lecturer in Physical Education in the School of Education at Roehampton University. He has co- and single-authored five publications in the field of physical education. His contribution to *Creative Approaches to Physical Education* brings to bear his experience and commitment to a developmental approach to teaching PE in primary schools, a personal philosophy that has underpinned thirty years of practice and teaching of the subject across all age groups, from toddlers to octogenarians.

Patrick Smith is Principal Lecturer and Programme Leader for Secondary Undergraduate Teacher Training at the University of Cumbria. He has almost thirty years' experience of teaching PE in secondary schools, further and higher education. He was an accredited team inspector for schools on behalf of Ofsted from 1997 to 2006 and has provided numerous staff development courses and conferences for teachers.

Glenn Swindlehurst currently works for Lancashire County Council as a teacher adviser for primary PE and is a primary PE specialist who has worked as a PE subject leader in a number of primary schools across the north-west of England. Glenn is the lead trainer for Lancashire Local Delivery Agency and an associate tutor for Edge Hill University. His main interests are developing dance across the curriculum, using ICT in primary PE to support learning and teaching, delivery of fundamental movement skills and developing ways of supporting the teaching of other subject learning outcomes through physical activity.

Acknowledgements

My wholehearted thanks go to Cathie Sanderson for all her invaluable help, patience and encouragement in the writing and editing of this book.

Foreword

When young people engage in good physical education they learn more than the physical. Well taught, they learn more about themselves as people, how to contribute to a bigger community and how to use skills in different contexts across the curriculum.

The book explores the way in which learning in physical education can be approached in an imaginative way as youngsters cross the primary–secondary divide. It gives ideas, suggestions and structures but also focuses upon seeing learning through the eyes of the pupil, recognising what engages, challenges and inspires. The insights in the book have implications for all other areas of the curriculum.

Children need basics in learning. They need to run free, to be outdoors, to have adventures, to stretch themselves, to dance, to play, to invent and to enjoy themselves – learning needs to be 'full of body felt' – and PE leads the way.

In turn, teachers need to enjoy the possibilities that this book offers. Crossing the primary to secondary divide in PE? Use the creative approaches in this book and it can be done . . . in one bound!

Mick Waters
Director of Curriculum
Qualifications and Curriculum Authority

Preface

The motivation for this book lay in the personal belief that PE should be a creative process, not merely a replication of some sort of body of knowledge. As a subject, PE has the potential to allow both teachers and pupils enormous scope for creative endeavour. The process of creativity is difficult to define but is generally accepted to be worthwhile and valuable to the individuals concerned. It is clear that this potential has not yet been fully explored within PE. Pleasingly, the value of PE to the school as a whole is now being recognised. This book is well timed; the new Key Stage 3 Programme of Study includes creativity as one of the four key concepts, and creativity in education is now being recognised as a key aspect of developing creative industries. These are seen as vital to the nation's prosperity. A refocus on creativity across the curriculum is essential, and in my view PE should play its full part in this initiative.

This book aims to raise awareness of the importance of taking a creative approach and provides an overview of the way creative approaches can be applied across the PE spectrum. It includes:

- an explanation of the way creativity is expected to be part of the whole curriculum;
- examples of creative teaching approaches in specific areas of the PE curriculum; and
- starting points for teachers to develop their own creative teaching approaches to PE.

The examples provided have been developed in schools and refined through practical experience. During this process one powerful theme has emerged: children enjoy working with creative teachers. They learn most with teachers who stimulate, challenge and change their thinking. Creative teachers respect pupils and individuals and maintain a very positive classroom ethos.

The book includes chapters on games; dance; gymnastics; outdoor and adventurous activities; PE and information and communications technology (ICT); the promotion of healthy, active lifestyles; and cross-curricular approaches. I hope it shows that there are boundless possibilities inherent within the many components of the subject. However, far from being an 'instruction manual', the aim of the book is to encourage teachers to continue to develop their own personal approach to creative teaching.

The book takes as its focus the teaching of PE to pupils in Key Stages 2 and 3. During Key Stage 1 they will have acquired basic movement skills essential to the development of creative ideas. There is a commonality between Key Stage 2 and 3 in the PE Programme of Study. The development of creative and critical thinking that takes place between the ages of 7 and 14 years is fertile ground for creative approaches.

The contributors to the book come from a range of backgrounds and experience. However, they are all characterised by one common feature: they are all creative teachers who believe in the potential of PE to unlock the creativity inherent in our pupils. The subtitle of this book is 'helping children to achieve their true potential', because a creative approach can help pupils of all abilities to achieve success.

Teachers already value creativity. How many times have we been surprised and pleased by an original and creative thought or action by one of our pupils? Creative teachers are characterised by several traits: they are able to see alternatives; they can often modify their situation to achieve their goals; they have a 'can do' attitude rather than finding reasons not to attempt a new teaching approach or curriculum innovation; and they have the flair and ability to play with ideas and are adaptable and flexible enough to change depending on the response of the children. Does this describe you? If so, this book will help you to continue to challenge the pupils – and yourself.

Jim Lavin
University of Cumbria
15 August 2007

Chapter 1

The creative agenda and its relationship to physical education

Jim Lavin

The notion of creativity has been a consistent focus of government initiatives over recent years. The National Advisory Committee on Creative and Cultural Education (NACCCE) was established in 1998, and its 1999 report, *All Our Futures: Creativity, Culture and Education*, set the framework for future developments.

The report stated that it was 'essential to provide opportunities for young people to express their own ideas, values and feelings'. It was felt that a key task for teachers was to help young people understand the process of creative thought production. Furthermore, there was recognition of the notion of 'emotional intelligence' (Goleman 1996), identified as the ability to understand, express and use our feelings and intuition.

At the same time, the Qualifications and Curriculum Authority (QCA) and the Department for Education and Employment (DfEE) identified 'creative thinking skills' as a key skill in the National Curriculum (DfEE and QCA 1999a, b). The then Secretary of State for Education and Skills asked the QCA to follow this up by investigating how schools could promote pupils' creativity through the National Curriculum. The QCA's creativity project focused on Key Stages 1, 2 and 3 and worked with 120 schools to investigate how they could develop pupils' creativity. The results of the project were published as *Creativity: Find It, Promote It* (2004), a report which provided practical materials and examples for developing creativity in schools. The QCA promotes creativity as an integral part of all National Curriculum subjects, and this report identified the characteristics of creative thinking and behaviour, including:

- questioning and challenging conventions and assumptions;
- making inventive connections and associating things that are not usually related;
- envisaging what might be, imagining and seeing things in the mind's eye;
- trying alternatives and fresh approaches, and keeping options open; and
- reflecting critically on ideas, actions and outcomes.

Other kinds of initiatives have flowed from these major developments. One such initiative is Creative Partnerships, a government-funded national initiative designed to build sustainable relationships between schools, creative individuals and organisations in thirty-six of the most disadvantaged areas in England. It aims to transform:

- the aspirations and achievements of young people;
- the approaches and attitudes of teachers and schools; and

- the practices of creative practitioners and organisations who wish to work in schools.

Some teachers in areas of social deprivation may be familiar with its work.

In 2003 the DfES published the document *Excellence and Enjoyment* for primary school teachers. Among other aspects, teachers were encouraged to develop creative approaches and to plan and respond to pupils' creative ideas and actions. It stated that 'promoting creativity is a powerful way of engaging pupils with their learning'. Furthermore, teachers were exhorted to 'take ownership of the curriculum . . . teachers have much more freedom than they often realise to design the timetable and decide what and how they teach'.

The Office for Standards in Education (Ofsted) carried out a survey identifying good practice in the promotion of creativity in schools (*Expecting the Unexpected: Developing Creativity in Primary and Secondary Schools*, Ofsted 2003). They found that there was generally high quality in creative work. Any barriers to creativity that existed could be overcome if teachers were committed to the notion of creativity and possessed good subject knowledge and a sufficiently broad range of pedagogic skills to foster creativity in all pupils, whatever their ability. Ofsted emphasised that 'the creativity observed in pupils is not associated with a radical new pedagogy . . . but with a willingness to observe, listen and work closely with children to help them develop their ideas in a purposeful way'.

In terms of PE, it was interesting that the report cited only one aspect of the PE curriculum. This related to a gymnastics lesson in a primary school, in which the use of mats in different colours and mathematical shapes prompted pupils to think about shapes in movement.

These initiatives have been further extended by the report *Nurturing Creativity in Young People* (Roberts 2006). This was jointly commissioned by the Department of Culture, Media and Sport (DCMS) and the Department for Education and Skills (DfES). The report set out what more the government could do to nurture young people's creativity, providing a clear framework for the further development of creativity for children and young people. This included:

- Creative portfolios – develop a personal portfolio, incorporating both formal and informal learning. This would support routes into the creativity sector.
- Early years – ensure the visibility of creativity in the early learning goal and in the guidance for children's centres.
- Extended schools – set explicit expectations and incentives for creative activity in extended schools built on best practice in personalised learning and in partnership with appropriate specialist schools.
- Building schools for the future (BSF) – create spaces for creativity and community use (linked to the community role of specialist schools). This would also involve young people in creating the design specification of BSF programmes.
- Leading creative learning – prepare new entrants to the education workforce for the roles involved in developing partnerships with creative organisations.
- Practitioner partnerships – create training, accreditation and recognition for creative practitioners.

- Pathways to creative industries – create links between course providers and industry practitioner networks, challenging industries to provide placement schemes.

The report also encouraged Ofsted to recognise creativity through self-evaluation and through the inclusion of creativity as one of the themes for the national review programme.

The reorganisation of the Department of Employment and Skills into the Department of Children, Schools and Families (DCSF) in June 2007 does not appear to have affected these developments and this report will remain as the template for the development of government thinking in this area for the foreseeable future.

Maisuria (2005) takes a more longitudinal view of creativity. Since the introduction of the National Curriculum, it has been felt that the plethora of centralised testing regimes and quality assurance measures have not only damaged the esteem of pupils and teachers but also turned education into the art of passing exams. The moves to reintroduce creativity were seen as being 'bolted on' to the National Curriculum, with the aim of re-energising teachers' and pupils' creative spirits.

I think most teachers of PE would feel, however, that the subject has been free from the pressures of testing and league tables that have applied to the core subjects.

Of course, good teachers have always been teaching in a creative way. Jones and Wyse (2004) suggest that creativity 'should be a characteristic of an approach to the curriculum which values every child's interests and styles of learning and encourages them to use their skills in new contexts'.

The nature of creativity in school

Here it is important to make the distinction between *creative teaching* and *teaching for creativity*. Creative teaching is seen as 'using imaginative approaches to make learning more interesting and effective' (NACCCE 1999). Craft (2005) proposes that the features of creative teaching could be innovation, relevance, control and ownership.

Teaching for creativity, by contrast, is seen as a form of teaching that is intended to develop young people's own creative thinking or behaviour (NACCCE 1999). There are also further distinctions to be made. The *Creativity: Find It, Promote It* (QCA 2004) document defines creativity as having the distinct characteristics of:

- imagination;
- purpose;
- originality; and
- value

Based on the QCA research, the document claims that creativity improves pupils' self-esteem, motivation and achievement in the following ways:

- pupils become more interested in discovering things for themselves;
- pupils become more open to new ideas;
- pupils become keen to work with others to explore ideas; and

- pupils become willing to work beyond lesson time when pursuing an idea or vision.

(QCA 2004)

The relationship of physical education to creativity

In terms of creativity, the focus of this book is placed on teaching PE at Key Stages 2 and 3. This is because of the commonality of the Key Stages in terms of the National Curriculum for PE and for the progression of creative and critical thinking that takes place between the ages of 7 and 14 years.

At Key Stage 2, the National Curriculum for PE (NCPE) has never particularly emphasised a creative approach, either in terms of creative teaching or creative learning. Pupils have been asked to acquire and develop skills; select and apply skills, tactics and compositional ideas; evaluate and improve performance; and have a knowledge and understanding of fitness and health. The only aspects in the programmes of study that relate to creativity have been in dance, games and gymnastics.

Even in outdoor and adventurous activities there has been no requirement to develop a creative approach. Pupils have been expected to use problem-solving skills, but that is very different from the creative process. The NACCCE recognised this: 'creativity and problem solving are not the same thing. Not all problems call for creative solutions or original thinking. Some can be solved routinely and logically. And not all creative thinking is directed to solving problems' (NACCCE 1999).

The importance of creative approaches was recognised in the launch of the revised Key Stage 3 National Curriculum in July 2007. The Chief Executive of QCA (2007) said: 'By mixing tradition with a more creative approach to the curriculum, we will achieve our objective of producing successful learners, confident individuals and responsible citizens' (www.qca.org.uk/qca_12195.aspx).

One of the four key concepts in the new secondary National Curriculum for PE at Key Stage 3 is creativity. Pupils need to understand the concept of creativity to be able to:

- deepen and broaden their knowledge, skills and understanding;
- use imaginative ways to express and communicate ideas, solve problems and overcome challenges; and
- explore and experiment with techniques, tactics and compositional ideas to produce efficient and effective outcomes.

Physical education teachers' understanding of creativity

Many of us have differing and sometimes conflicting understandings of the term 'creativity'. My experience of talking to secondary PE colleagues is that many think that creativity is bound up with notions of dance and the arts and is separate from areas such as games, swimming and athletics, which depend on developing skills and techniques. Some see certain pupils as being creative but feel that not all pupils have this capacity, while others see it as irrelevant to the core principle of teaching PE; that is, viewing PE as knowledge, skills and understanding, without making the connection to creativity.

Certainly, the creative approach presents a challenge to those of us who have come from a tradition of teaching accepted orthodox techniques and skills in a sports-related context. Many of us have undertaken coaching awards that focus on the development of skill through a canon of coaching manuals and approaches detailing how to hold a hockey stick, receive a ball, deliver a top spin forehand, and so on. The creative approach may be seen as presenting ideas that do not fall into the accepted ways of teaching physical activity and presenting ideas that could challenge the status quo between teacher and pupil.

Every child is capable of being creative. However, when pupils are forced to suppress their creativity by participating in an activity they dislike or which does not motivate them, then their response can lead to inappropriate behaviour. At its best, creative activity in PE should provide a learning environment in which pupils are relaxed and perform the activity with enjoyment. Smiles and laughter can often accompany attempts to find a creative solution to an issue. PE, perhaps more than many other subjects, has the potential to provide pupils with moments of high achievement, even joy. This is very different from the situation where we follow a prescribed format that we have taught many times before with the pupils following a rigid, predetermined pathway in gaining skills that they perhaps feel have little relevance to them.

Some of us may have difficulty with teaching aspects of PE that do not have preordained outcomes. There are those of us who need to have control, who need to feel that our teaching is organised and ordered. Some of us are wary about organising too much collaborative work. This kind of approach can be viewed as time consuming and even worse, in a PE context, not very active, at least during the planning/discussion phase. However, not all PE needs to be taught this way. It clearly has its place among a range of other teaching methods, but need not be the pre-eminent way to teach PE.

Kilbourne (1998), a dance/creative movements teacher, reported that his secondary undergraduate PE majors frequently displayed the least amount of creativity in their final dance performances in comparison with science, biology and elementary (primary) specialists. He analysed the possible roots of creative deficiency in PE and found that the PE students had been fed a diet of formalised coaching instruction in which all personal decisions had been removed other than to play to the coaches' demands. This is perhaps more typical of the American system, where high-level performers are given formal coaching from a very young age, than of the British experience. Perhaps the lack of creativity in the NCPE since its inception has given us a generation of PE teachers with little or no personal experience of how to develop creativity within the PE curriculum.

Teaching styles appropriate to the creativity agenda

Some of you may have developed differing teaching styles in order to undertake creative teaching. For the purpose of analysing the style used in the teaching of PE it would be helpful to use the spectrum devised by Mosston and Ashworth (2002). They identified that the most commonly used teaching styles in PE were the command and the practice style. In the command style the teacher makes *all* the decisions and the learners have to follow the exact directions of the teacher in order to achieve success. In the practice style, the teacher makes *most* of the decisions. He or she instructs the learner in the technique required and the learner then practises the technique. The learner makes some decisions during this practice phase but seeks approval from the teacher that these decisions are correct.

Clearly, these styles would not allow creative learning to take place because the learner's role is to do as they are told as directed by the teacher.

There are other styles to consider. Within the guided discovery style, the teacher plans a learning outcome and systematically leads the learner to discover the outcome. This allows the pupils to feel they are discovering concepts and approaches, though it is still not creative learning in its fullest sense, as the teacher still determines the outcome.

To fully engage with creative learning the divergent style would be more appropriate. Here, the teacher presents questions or a problem situation and pupils are invited to discover an alternative solution. The pupils contribute to decisions at all stages since their responses may determine the next move.

Interestingly, some of the QCA case studies (QCA 2004) on creative learning involved both teachers and pupils working together as joint learners. A topic or focus was chosen and the teachers concerned acknowledged that this was an area in which they had little knowledge. Both teachers and pupils were joint learners and the teachers were confident enough to allow the pupils to lead the process.

Craft (2005) identifies a dilemma that many teachers may face. When confronted with a pupil exhibiting creative behaviour, they may feel that the pupil is being deviant or even naughty. Those teachers who seek to promote creativity may have to accept that this creativity may threaten the existing rules, behaviour and order:

> Clearly, teachers' own professional judgements will dictate the balance between the maintenance of and the challenge to the status quo; but if creativity is to be truly creative and to offer opportunities for 'out of the box' thinking, then our classrooms and schools must indeed offer this balance, and not simply opportunities for recreating what is already known.
>
> (Craft 2005)

For primary teachers who do not have a specialist knowledge of PE, the creative agenda may offer an alternative approach. Some primary teachers often feel inadequate in teaching PE because of lack of subject knowledge. Some say, 'I cannot teach this sport because I don't know the rules and skills involved'. However, unlike their secondary colleagues, primary teachers have the advantage of knowing the children extremely well. Therefore, given careful reflection, learning opportunities can be devised in which the children lead the process of discovery about aspects of PE. This could relate to developing an appropriate exercise programme or the invention of a new game that challenges and includes all the pupils. In this way, lack of subject knowledge is not a problem, as the ideas or solutions (or knowledge) come from the child, not from the teacher.

Chedzoy (2005) has provided a very useful overview on ways in which the six areas of PE taught at Key Stage 2 could be adapted to include creative learning. From this work, it is clear that the approach applies equally well across the range of the National Curriculum for PE, even in those areas such as swimming and athletics which are traditionally taught through a skills-based approach. The approach advocated by Chedzoy could work equally well at Key Stage 3, given suitable adjustments for ability levels.

The distinction between creative teachers and creative learners in the physical education context

Some teachers are creative about the way they teach. They have developed initiatives such as bringing in professional sportspeople to work with the pupils, introduced a new sport to the pupils, or devised a new dance routine or exercise programme.

However, this is very different from promoting pupils' creative thinking and behaviour. This relies on the teacher being innovative in the way he or she allows pupils room to develop their own ideas and approaches.

Teachers can promote creativity in PE by:

- Planning specific schemes of work that give pupils opportunity to be creative. This can apply across the PE curriculum.
- Looking for opportunities to promote creative responses in existing schemes of work and lesson plans. Can pupils be creative in undertaking a unit of work on football or netball? Certainly the existing skills they have will give them a firm base on which to develop and carry out ideas.
- Using a range of learning styles; for example, use of stimuli in dance, visual materials such as diagrams and DVDs, small group discussions and collaboration.
- Limiting time, scale or resources. Constraints can stimulate new ways of working and improvisation. The constraints already existing in most schools (such as a limited range of PE equipment, limited amount of time and lack of space) can be turned into a stimulus for creativity.
- Moving towards the use of a more cross-curricular approach at both Key Stages 2 and 3. This can be used to give pupils a wider vision of the place of exercise and sport in society. For example, working with design and technology, and information and communications technology could provide a creative stimulus to the practical nature of PE.
- Setting clear learning objectives and building specific creativity objectives into planning. This can be integrated with specific PE objectives. You may wish to develop the pupils' tactical awareness in games or to explore compositional ideas.

Do pupils need prior learning in order to be creative?

The short answer to this is yes. The QCA's creativity project (QCA 2004) found that teachers realised that creativity does not happen in a vacuum. Pupils need subject-specific knowledge and skills for their creativity to flourish. For those who see the role of PE in terms of developing fitness skills competence and performance this may come as something of a relief. There needs to be a firm foundation of physical skills in order for creativity to flourish. Just as pupils can feel that they cannot master the skills involved to play a sport effectively (such as tennis, where repeated failure to keep the ball in court can lead to giving up any attempt to continue in the sport), so pupils could abandon a promising creative approach because it is deemed too hard or beyond their capabilities.

On the other hand, lack of variety and too much emphasis on a particular activity can cause creativity to diminish. I recall asking a group of trainee teachers in an American university to devise a striking/fielding game. Because the only striking/fielding game they had played since the age of 7 was softball/baseball, they were unable to devise anything other than slight variations of the baseball concept.

Alternative approaches to learning

The growing obesity rates and sedentary lifestyles of a proportion of the 7- to 14-year-old population is a concern to the PE teaching profession (Jotangia *et al.* 2005). Within the 2000–2007 National Curriculum for PE there was little scope or encouragement for teachers to use creative approaches in order to develop strategies that would seek to ameliorate the drop-off in physical activity experienced during Key Stage 3, particularly among teenage girls. However, the introduction of the new Key Stage 3 PE curriculum, with creativity as one of the key concepts, allows for more imaginative and innovative programmes to be developed. The focus on creativity reinforces the need for greater variety and approaches in the teaching of the PE curriculum offered to pupils aged 7 to 14. The 'staple diet' of the traditional team games still serves to provide enjoyable competition and skill development. However, perhaps the PE curriculum should reflect the leisure interests of our society more closely. The creative agenda could spur us into developing a wider view of what PE is. The pedagogical imperative to introduce children to a wide range of physical learning experiences could mean that we see activities such as yoga, martial arts, cycling and skateboarding as a normal and accepted part of the PE curriculum. It must be acknowledged here that some innovative schools already offer this (QCA 2004).

The introduction of the revised programmes of study at Key Stage 3 in September 2008 offers another opportunity for creative initiatives in PE. One aim of the review is: 'improving coherence, highlighting commonalities between the key concepts at the heart of each subject, encouraging links between areas of the curriculum and reducing the overall level of prescription' (QCA 2007).

In other words, PE is being encouraged to link with other subjects on areas of common interest. There is a great deal of scope here for us to work collaboratively with other primary subject leaders or colleagues in other secondary subject areas. The possibilities are exciting. At the secondary level it would allow teachers to see pupils as a whole rather than just learners in their own subject. At primary level, although cross-curricular approaches have been a feature of the curriculum for many years, the possibilities offered by PE have been generally unrecognised. The creative agenda, with its emphasis on collaborative learning, provides us with a springboard to develop themes and approaches that would link PE with other subjects in a meaningful way, providing stimulating teaching and learning opportunities.

The Physical Education, School Sport and Club Links Strategy (DfES/DCMS 2002) has a role to play here. The role of the school sports coordinator (SSCo) in developing the PE curriculum provision has been of enormous benefit to primary schools. The SSCo could certainly act as the catalyst for change in helping non-specialist primary teachers to adopt a more creative PE curriculum.

This process should match the need, identified in the new Key Stage 3 provision, to make informed choices about healthy active lifestyles by identifying the types of activities that pupils are best suited to. However, there is a balance to be found in offering pupils greater choice while ensuring that real learning and progression takes place. The 'taster' approach needs to be avoided.

The creative process advocated in this chapter is summarised in Figure 1.1.

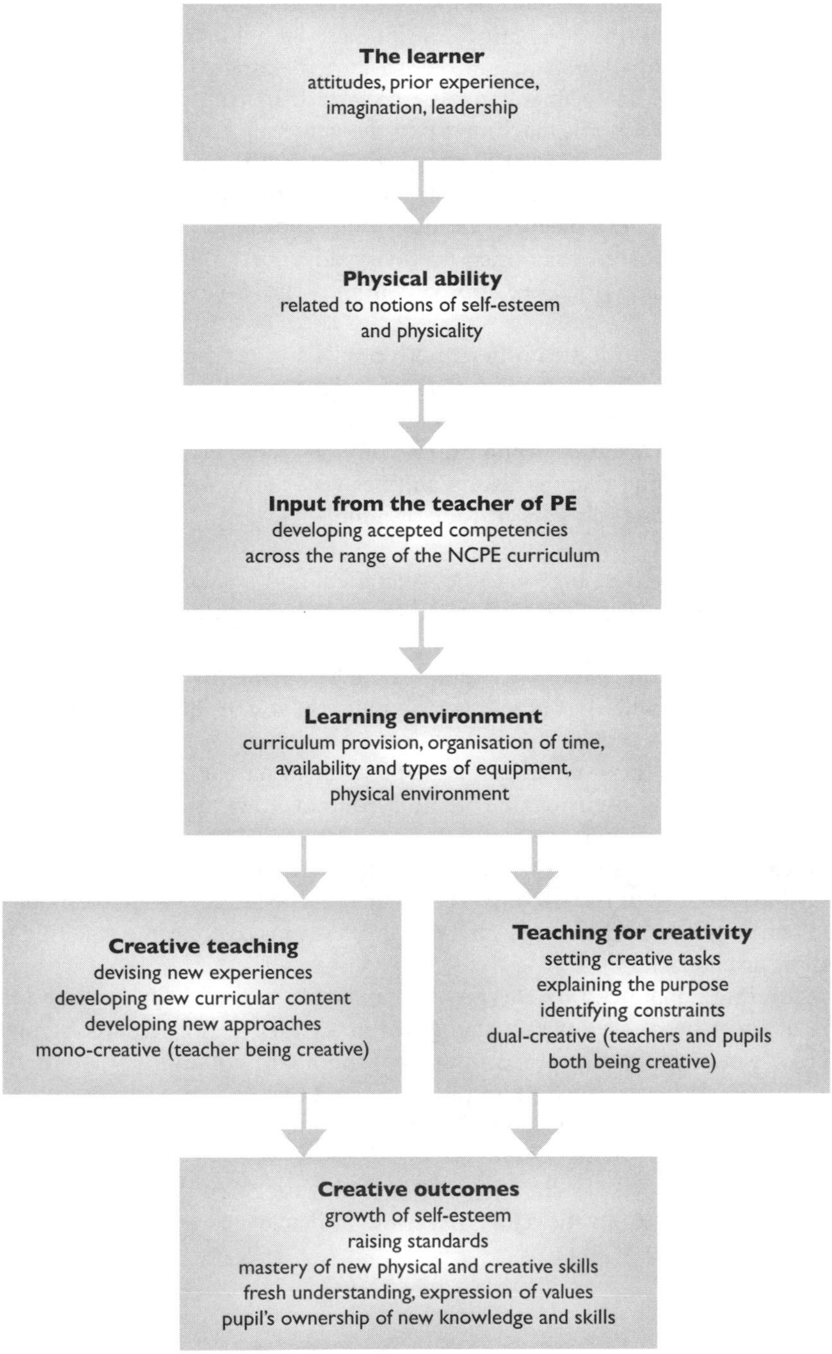

The learner
attitudes, prior experience,
imagination, leadership

↓

Physical ability
related to notions of self-esteem
and physicality

↓

Input from the teacher of PE
developing accepted competencies
across the range of the NCPE curriculum

↓

Learning environment
curriculum provision, organisation of time,
availability and types of equipment,
physical environment

↓

Creative teaching
devising new experiences
developing new curricular content
developing new approaches
mono-creative (teacher being creative)

Teaching for creativity
setting creative tasks
explaining the purpose
identifying constraints
dual-creative (teachers and pupils
both being creative)

↓

Creative outcomes
growth of self-esteem
raising standards
mastery of new physical and creative skills
fresh understanding, expression of values
pupil's ownership of new knowledge and skills

Figure 1.1 The creative continuum in physical education.

The acceptance of creative approaches

I can imagine some colleagues thinking, with some resignation or even indignation, 'not another initiative that we have to follow, imposed on us from above'.

It would be a pity if this perception continued to be held and the creativity agenda was blocked, played down or even ignored. Despite the range of educational initiatives over recent years, PE has been relatively unaffected. In fact, curriculum change has been slow, with many schools teaching PE in the way they have done for a number of years. It could be that the time is right to recognise that the old certainties about the traditional PE curriculum no longer apply, and teaching styles and learning methods need to change if we are to meet the needs of our children.

Ofsted (2003) reported that one secondary advanced skills teacher (AST) with responsibility for PE described her approach in the following way:

> I try to be an inspiration to others, both pupils and teachers. There's no point in doing the same things the same way day in and day out. You become too predictable. You need routines, but I try to adapt and be flexible in my content and to look for different ways of doing things with different classes. You need to have a fresh eye and I think there is always another way, perhaps another approach. I try to surprise my classes. It's an attitude of mind!

Controlled, managed change is to be welcomed, and teachers should not feel that this change is a threat (Figure 1.1). As Ted Wragg (2005) said,

> That does not mean that every lesson should be a fresh invention – you cannot do it, you'd kill yourself. Teaching is a busy job; you've got lots of things to do.

Moreover, he makes the point that far from teachers having to devise new ways of teaching or developing their own curriculum content, they often use approaches and material that are from other sources.

The creativity agenda does involve risk and if a teacher tries a new idea or approach they may have no idea of its outcome. It may be that the idea needs to be modified and adapted before it is judged a success, but the alternative is to continue teaching without innovation or change.

New funding announced by the government in July 2007 will provide for up to 5 hours of sport per week for our young people by 2010, through a combination of sport provision in the curriculum and out-of-school and community activities (Sport England 2007). Although this funding is earmarked for the promotion of competitive sport, the extra time is to be welcomed in providing more time and space for teachers to innovate.

Perhaps the last word should be given to Ted Wragg (2005). When asked about creativity in the classroom, he said, 'My view is that every teacher should have an obligation to invent'.

References

Chedzoy, S. (2005) 'Children, Creativity and Physical Education', in Wilson, A. (ed.), *Creativity in Primary Education*. Exeter: Learning Matters.

Craft, A. (2005) *Creativity in Schools: Tensions and Dilemmas.* Abingdon: Routledge.

DfEE and QCA (1999a) *The National Curriculum Handbook for Teachers in Key Stages 1 and 2.* London: Qualifications and Curriculum Authority.

DfEE and QCA (1999b) *The National Curriculum Handbook for Teachers in Key Stages 3 and 4.* London: Qualifications and Curriculum Authority.

DfES (2003) *Excellence and Enjoyment: A Strategy for Primary Schools.* London: Department for Education and Skills.

DfES/DCMS (2002) *Learning through PE and Sport: An update on the National PE, School Sport and Club Links Strategy.* London: Department for Education and Skills.

Goleman, D. (1996) *Emotional Intelligence: Why It Can Matter More than IQ.* London: Bloomsbury.

Jones, R. and Wyse, D. (2004) *Creativity in the Primary Curriculum.* London: David Fulton Publishers Ltd.

Jotangia, D., Moody, A., Stamctakis, E. and Wardle, H. (2005) *Obesity among Children under 11.* London: National Centre for Social Research.

Kilbourne, J. (1998) 'Rebuilding the Bridge between Physical Education and Creativity', *The Journal of Physical Education, Recreation and Dance,* May, 25–31.

Maisuria, A. (2005) 'The Turbulent Times of Creativity in the National Curriculum', *Policy Futures in Education,* 3(2): 141–152.

Mosston, M. and Ashworth, S. (2002) *Teaching Physical Education.* New York: Macmillan.

National Advisory Committee on Creative and Cultural Education (1999) *All Our Futures: Creativity, Culture and Education.* London: Department for Education and Employment.

Ofsted (2003) *Expecting the Unexpected: Developing Creativity in Primary and Secondary Schools.* London: Ofsted.

QCA (2004) *Creativity: Find It, Promote It.* London: Qualifications and Curriculum Authority.

QCA (2007) *Secondary Curriculum Review Statutory Consultation: Draft Summary of Findings.* London: Qualifications and Curriculum Authority. Available online at www.qca.org.uk/curriculum.

Roberts, P. (2006) *Nurturing Creativity in Young People.* London: Department for Culture, Media and Sport and Department for Education and Skills.

Sport England (2007) 'Sport England Welcomes Investment into Schools and School Club Links', press release, 13 July.

Wood, P. and Jeffrey, B. (1996) *Teachable Moments: The Art of Creative Teaching in Primary Schools.* Buckingham: Open University Press.

Wragg, T. (2005) 'Going against the Flow: An Interview with Ted Wragg', in Wilson, A. (ed.), *Creativity in Primary Education.* Exeter: Learning Matters.

Chapter 2

Creative games at Key Stages 2 and 3

Moving the goal posts

Jim Lavin

Games continue to have a pre-eminence in the National Curriculum for PE. It is the only aspect that is required to be taught from Key Stage 1 to Key Stage 4. The Physical Education, School Sport and Club Links (PESSCL) Strategy (DfES/DCMS 2002) has continued to develop the idea of competitive school sport. However, it could be argued that although there has been a range of developments in the way PE is structured (e.g. increased use of coaches in primary schools, the role of school sports coordinators and sports colleges, the development of competition managers) the actual content of games teaching at Key Stages 2 and 3 has changed very little. Games continue to be taught in the traditional way. A warm-up is followed by a skills session that is then put into a games situation. Furthermore, the way PE has been taught has changed very little. Physical education teachers continue, on the whole, to use the instructional model of teaching. This is, of course, very effective in terms of time and resources. There is also, however, much innovative practice taking place within the profession. The teaching of games for understanding (Thorpe, Bunker and Almond 1986) has certainly made an impact on the delivery of games in secondary schools. Many schools are looking to extend their PE curriculum and offer a wider range of activities.

This chapter examines the possibilities offered by the creative model to teaching games. It uses two approaches within this model to provide a framework for games development. The first is *teaching for creativity*. This approach focuses on the children's creative powers. Pupils are encouraged by the teacher to think of creative solutions to games situations. The teacher does not seek to provide answers for the pupils but allows them to develop their own creative ideas. They act as a facilitator and guide. The process of creative thinking is seen as more important than the end product. The second approach, *creative teaching*, is based on teachers of PE using imaginative approaches to make learning more interesting and effective. It is based on a broad definition of what constitutes PE. The inclusion of a particular activity is based on its physicality and value to the pupil. The notion of educating pupils for lifelong physical activity strongly influences the inclusion of activities in this category.

Part 1: the teaching for creativity approach

Before undertaking the teaching for creativity approach, pupils should have a sound vocabulary of movement skills. The experience of physical development in the foundation stage followed by experience of the Programme of Study for games at Key Stage 1 should enable pupils to undertake creative learning with confidence. These key skills are:

- travel with a ball and other equipment in different ways;
- send a ball and other equipment in different ways;
- receive a ball and other equipment in different ways;
- develop these skills in a game situation;
- play simple competitive games in the three aspects of games: net, striking/fielding and invasion; and
- use simple tactics for attacking and defending.

It is fortunate that a greater focus has recently been placed on pupils gaining their basic vocabulary of movement. The basic moves approach (Jess and Dewar 2004) would provide a developmentally appropriate introduction to games skills that would allow children to be technically mature, adaptable and creative.

For Key Stage 2 pupils the approach should form part of a 'games spiral' that allows the pupils to experience formal games across the invasion, striking/fielding and net continuum in terms of simplified versions of recognised games. They should re-visit these games after the teaching for creativity input.

In addition, the 'planning, modifying and identifying next steps' element inherent in the development of creative approaches to games is part of the 'discussion and group interaction' strand in the framework for planning in *Teaching, Speaking and Listening in Key Stages 1 and 2*, QCA/99/391 (QCA 1999).

Key Stage 3 pupils will already have a broad understanding of the structure of the major games involved in the invasion, striking/fielding and net spectrum. For these pupils the teaching for creativity approach will allow them to transfer many of the games skills already learnt into new and challenging situations.

Implementation at Key Stage 2

This approach should be seen as requiring a careful progression and development of the children's skills and creative abilities. It would be easy to put them into a situation where they were presented with too much, too early.

Progression

Numbers of players: individual activities; partner activities; small team (three or four pupils); larger team (five or six pupils, maximum). It is better to play uneven team games before moving onto games with even numbers in each team. This allows players more time for decision-making in terms of passing and more time in preparing to shoot/score.

Playing space

From limited space to the use of more space in relation to the group size, depending on the facilities and space available in the school.

Equipment

The use of limited equipment to the use of varied and more challenging equipment.

Rules

From simple rules to more complex rules as the group size and types of equipment increase.

Skills

From simple skills to more complex skills as the game is developed.

There are a number of starting points for the development of creative games, including:

- games equipment;
- techniques or skills; and
- tactics or strategies.

Equipment-led creative games

Years 3 and 4

Prior to the lesson or unit of work prepare laminated cards with three pieces of games equipment listed on them. Lay out the games apparatus so that it is easy for the pupils to access it.

Divide the pupils into pairs. Give them a space to work in. This could be marked by lines in the playground or areas delineated by cones. They pick a card from a central place, select the equipment on the card and move back into their space.

An alternative would be to allow them to choose two or three pieces of equipment in turn. This gives them more ownership of the learning process, but they may choose games equipment that poses too difficult a task in developing their games. You can monitor this and make adjustments according to their creative ability.

Stage 1

This approach should be undertaken over a period of several weeks. A half-term is a useful period of time to allow the learning to take place.

Explain the purpose and value of the teaching for creativity approach to the pupils. These include:

1 Constructing a game that is theirs, something that they have made and created. It will be unique to them.
2 Discovering for themselves why rules are important and what purpose they serve.
3 Being involved in their own learning. They should not rely on the teacher to tell them what to do. In this sense they are independent learners.
4 Sharing their ideas with others. They should listen to the ideas of others. They should work together cooperatively to develop the game.
5 Communicating effectively with each other and with the teacher. They will need to articulate the reasoning and purpose of the games and explain how the game developed in the testing of ideas period.

6   Teaching other members of their group, other groups and their teacher.
7   Working and playing safely (pupils may need reminding here of some basic safety points, such as no physical contact games, no games which involve using pupils as targets, notions of enough space, and safe use of equipment).

Stage 2

It would be easy to allow pupils free choice of equipment, size of area and number of participants. However, experience has shown that this is not effective with pupils of their age. They will use too much equipment, devise games with very complicated rules or construct a game that is just an enjoyable low-level activity with little educational merit.

The pupils need to be provided with:

*   a distinct playing area; and
*   a limited number of pupils to each group. You should decide the composition of the group taking into account the personalities of the pupils. The groups should be six to eight pupils in size. Too small a group will rule out a team game approach, too large a group would mean too many children would be competing to be heard.

Stage 3

Outline the task. This is to devise a game in the context of the space available and using the equipment provided. The game should be safe, fair and enjoyable for all. Notions of inclusion can be introduced here. 'You are all stars' is the positive message to give, not focusing on one or two people in the group achieving at the expense of others. The grouping of pupils into equal ability groups would be helpful here.

It would be interesting to see whether the resulting games are cooperative or competitive. The rationale often advanced for games is that children are inherently competitive and that competition teaches children the hard facts of life, that of winning and losing and having to be competitive in order to succeed. In fact, my experience has been that children often develop cooperative activities where they work together to achieve a common goal.

The reality is that some children are very competitive, some others are fairly competitive and some children are just happy to take part and enjoy the experience. The teaching for creativity approach allows for individual expression in the pupils' approach to games-making in terms of their own competitiveness.

Explain to the pupils that each member of the group should think of a possible game. This stops the dominant members of the group from forcing their will on the others and dictating which games they want to play.

Stage 4

The pupils should have a period of play with the games equipment that has been given to them (5 minutes). You should ask them to find ways of using the equipment other than the 'normal'. For instance, if they have skipping ropes, ask them to find ways of using it other than skipping!

You could offer unusual combinations of equipment to challenge your pupils. Giving a group bats and balls would probably result in striking/fielding activities or net-type games. By pairing bats with bean bags or quoits, the pupils would be challenged to devise new ways of utilising the equipment.

After the initial play to discover the properties of the equipment you should ask the pupils to gather as a group and discuss possible ideas. They are allowed to try out an idea if it seems feasible to them to see if it works in practice. (By the end of the unit it is expected that each child will have come up with an idea. You need to monitor this. If a child cannot devise a game you can act as a facilitator to help them.)

There are several possibilities from here. Some groups will find an activity they enjoy and develop it. Other groups will find that an idea is either unsafe (you will need to monitor this carefully) or unworkable. In either event, they can sit down to discuss a new idea. The rule of everyone sitting down to discuss an idea is an important one. All too often children start to play with the equipment in ones and twos and do not work, listen or communicate as a group. The activity then degenerates into a free-play activity with little structure.

This process can continue over several lessons. If a group likes an idea they can start to develop it into a coherent game. Your role as the teacher is to act as a facilitator, asking open-ended questions and perhaps being a fellow learner, with the pupils teaching you. Occasionally, I take a pupil who is lacking in confidence or ideas to one side in private and explain a games concept to them, which they are then able to take back to the group as their idea in order to both stimulate the group and encourage some self-assurance in the child.

You should make a judgement about the uniqueness of the game. If it is too derivative of formal recognised games you should ask the group to begin again or to change the game.

Stage 5

Once a game idea has caught the pupils' imaginations, you could set the following tasks:

- decide on a set of rules;
- decide on a workable scoring system;
- identify specific techniques;
- identify specific roles within the game;
- decide on specific safety aspects; and
- ensure that the game is fully inclusive.

If the pupils are enthusiastic about the game concept they can continue to play it in order to develop the tactical capabilities of the game.

The group have now reached the stage when the game can be codified and written down. This could be a cross-curricular activity involving:

- information technology skills (e.g. use of video, interactive whiteboards and concept keyboards);
- design and technology skills (e.g. the development of specialist equipment);

- art (e.g. three-dimensional perspective drawing and figurative work);
- English (e.g. speaking and listening skills, descriptive writing); or
- mathematics (e.g. devising a scoring system and the possible measurement of a court/playing area).

Stage 6

Once a game has been developed sufficiently, each group should be given the opportunity of explaining it to others in the class and demonstrating how the game works. The whole class can then play the game in their own groups, coached by the originating players.

The expectation is that each group will produce at least one game that they can demonstrate to the rest of the class. Some productive groups can produce a number of games over the course of the unit of work. Part of the fun is finding an appropriate name for each game.

Stage 7

The culmination of the unit would be to have each group contribute a written record of their favourite game. This could either go into a class book of games or a classroom display.

EXAMPLE OF ACTUAL PRACTICE

One group of five was given skipping ropes (without handles) and hoops. They devised a game that required them to pass through the hoops that were linked by the ropes (as in a tunnel). Each player held a hoop, other than the one who was to pass through the tunnel created by the hoops. As soon as one person (player 5) had passed through all the hoops, he or she took the place of player 1, who moved to the next hoop. Player 2 moved to the hoop held by player 3, and so on. Player 4 was, then, the next one to go through the hoops. All the players had to go through the hoops and the process was timed. The competition was, therefore, to get all players through the hoops in the quickest possible time.

Stage 8

A variation for Years 5 and 6 would be to focus on a specific aspect of the games curriculum:

- invasion;
- striking/fielding; or
- net.

Skills- or technique-led creative games

In this model the pupils split into twos or threes (Years 3 and 4) or groups of seven or eight (Years 5 and 6).

Stage 1

The pupils are given cards that outline developmentally appropriate games skills and techniques. The skills and techniques could be:

- Catching – with two hands, both downward cradle and upward cradle.
- Throwing – both underarm and overarm, using a variety of objects.
- Kicking – different sizes and types of balls.
- Travelling with – using a variety of ways such as running with ball in hands, bouncing a ball, travelling with a ball on the ground (both round and oval), using an implement such as a hockey stick to move a ball.
- Striking – strike a ball or shuttlecock using a variety of implements including tennis rackets, rounders bats, softball bats, table tennis bats, badminton rackets or hockey sticks.
- Aiming – various types of balls using parts of the body or equipment such as hockey sticks, pop lacrosse sticks, tennis rackets or badminton rackets.
- Fielding – various types of balls at different heights and speed.
- Bowling – underarm as in rounders and softball, and overarm as in cricket.
- Passing – using different parts of the body such as hands and feet. Different types of passing such as long and short, different types of equipment such as footballs, netballs, hockey sticks or rugby balls.
- Receiving – a ball with different parts of the body: feet, thighs, hands, arms, chest and head. Receiving balls and other equipment at different heights and speeds. Receiving a ball or shuttlecock with hockey sticks, rackets or pop lacrosse sticks.
- Dribbling – using different-sized balls with feet and hands or with an implement like a hockey stick. This is different from travelling because quick turns and close control of the ball should be encouraged.

Stage 2

The pupils can select the cards that appeal to them. The number of cards allowed for each group could depend on the creative and physical ability of the group (you could monitor this and make discreet suggestions).

Stage 3

The pupils are given the opportunity to discuss how to create a game using the various skills they have selected. Each member of the group should come up with an idea. Some groups may ask you if they can have another skill card if it becomes apparent that their game would be improved by a different skill. They are also allowed to request games equipment that will enable them to perform the skills. You are looking for originality, so if a group requests a football in order to play an invasion-type game of kicking a ball into a goal it would be appropriate to ask them to come up with a more original idea.

Stage 4

The pupils try out the ideas they have developed. They should be encouraged to give everyone's idea a trial. Too often a pupil's idea can be dismissed as impractical at the discussion stage but the process of physically trying out the idea is a very valuable one. The reasons why a game may fail will lead to positive outcomes because mistakes will be avoided when other games are tried. The focus of the games should be on the skills chosen.

Stages 5, 6, 7 and 8

As with the equipment-led game approach.

Tactical or strategy-led games

This approach focuses on developing an awareness of tactics and strategies that are inherent in games. All of us will be familiar with the inappropriate pass in a rounders match; the bases are loaded and the fielder throws to first base! Likewise, how many games of football have we seen where all five members of the five-a-side team want to be Wayne Rooney and score all the goals? This approach of developing a game with appropriate team play and formations poses a challenge to pupils. It is an approach more suited to Years 5 and 6 when they will have had the opportunity to develop their games skills but are still not tactically aware.

Possible challenges

INVASION

Devise a five-a-side game, which requires all members of the team to both defend when the ball is lost and attack when the ball is gained. (Basketball is a good example of this type of game but the pupils should be encouraged to develop their own unique game.)

NET

Devise a five versus five net game in which the ball is not allowed to hit the floor. The court is not allowed to be rectangular. The net should be above the head height of the players. (This is a volleyball-type game but the skills of setting, smashing and digging are not expected.) The focus is on the players' awareness of covering the whole of the court between them and of deciding who is going to receive the ball or object sent over the net.

STRIKING/FIELDING

Devise a five versus five game that requires a ball to be struck and fielded. The teams cannot use a rounders/softball/cricket formation, in terms of running between bases or wickets. (This game requires the players to decide a new formation of bases or wickets.) The interesting aspect will be if they create a game that allows them to have five fielders able to run players out and also to be in a position to catch the batter out.

Implementation at Key Stage 3

The aim is to develop a concept of games-play through a teaching for creativity approach.

Learning outcomes for pupils

Pupils should be able to:

- understand the underlying structure of games-play through practical activity and experience;
- understand the need for rules within the context of games-play, incorporating concepts of fairness, tolerance and consideration for others;
- see the need for safety within a game rather than merely recite given safety rules; and
- develop game strategies related to the needs of the game.

Net/wall

1 Can you use a wall appropriately?
2 Height of barrier? What difference does the shape/height have to be? Does it always have to be a regular shape?
3 What equipment is appropriate and how should it be used? Do we always have to throw by hand?
4 Which techniques suit the game?
5 Is it safe?
6 Is it inclusive?
7 What scoring system and rules are appropriate for maximum enjoyment and skill level?
8 Can you develop appropriate tactics?

Develop a striking and fielding game

1 Consider the shape of the area. Where do players run to? Do they run at all?
2 Scoring systems.
3 Adaptation of equipment?
4 Which techniques suit the game?
5 Safety aspects?
6 Is it inclusive?
7 Can you develop appropriate tactics?

We do not want a modified version of softball or rounders.

Develop an invasion game

1 Consider the playing area. Does it always have to be a rectangular shape?
2 Consider how to develop the concept. Does an invasion game always have just two teams or could it have three or four?
3 What equipment would be suitable? Do you need equipment at all?
4 Consider the safety aspects.
5 Is it inclusive?
6 Which techniques suit the game?
7 Can you develop appropriate tactics?
8 Can you move away from kicking (football) or throwing/passing (netball, basketball, rugby) invasion games?

OPTION ONE

Divide the class into three groups. Each group takes one of the three areas. They develop their creative game over a period of two to three lessons, depending on their progress. They then share this with the other two groups (who play the game taught by the group). The process is repeated as below.

Lessons 1–3	Developing the game.
Lesson 4	Group 1 teaches its game to groups 2 and 3.
Lesson 5	Group 2 teaches its game to groups 1 and 3.
Lesson 6	Group 3 teaches its game to groups 1 and 2.

OPTION TWO

Divide the class into three groups. For the first two lessons, all pupils develop their version of an invasion game, then the process below is followed:

Lesson 3	Pupils demonstrate the games to each other.
Lessons 4 and 5	Pupils develop their version of a net game.
Lesson 6	Pupils demonstrate the games to each other.
Lessons 7 and 8	Pupils develop their version of a striking/fielding game.
Lesson 9	Pupils demonstrate their game to each other.

DEMONSTRATION LESSON ORGANISATION

Part 1	Group 1 teaches groups 2 and 3.
Part 2	Group 2 teaches groups 1 and 3.
Part 3	Group 3 teaches groups 1 and 2.

In each of these demonstration lessons the group teaching their game writes a lesson plan, drills and skills, gives out equipment, referees the game, keeps score and provides encouragement.

PRACTICAL EXAMPLE

When I taught this to a Year 8 class I asked one group to devise a net game. They chose to erect several landing mats (formerly known as crash mats) across the middle of a court. This meant that it was not possible to see the other team. The ball was thrown over the top of the mats and, therefore, the receiving team had very little time to respond before catching the ball. This caused them to focus on their reaction skills. The development of this was that one member from each side stood at the side of the court so that they could see the other side and direct the person throwing the ball to where they should throw the ball. The game, therefore, evolved into a volleyball-type game but with the added need to respond very quickly to the path and direction of the ball.

Part 2: creative teaching in physical education in Key Stages 2 and 3

In Part 1 of this chapter we examined ways in which the teacher could act as a facilitator to enable pupils to create their own games.

In this part, we will be examining another aspect of the creativity model. In this context it is the teacher who is the prime mover in introducing and encouraging physical activity that is outside the normal curriculum provision of most schools.

The approach holds many possibilities for learner and teacher alike. The pupils are provided with a much greater range of physical activities so their knowledge and understanding of physical education is deepened. The pupils are given opportunities to take part in activities that would not otherwise be available to many others. In this sense their experience of the possibilities of lifelong physical activity are enhanced because of their greater awareness of the benefits and range of physical activities available.

For the teacher this approach moves them away from the repetition involved in teaching basic games and sports skills to beginners. In my research with experienced PE teachers (Lavin 2001), they describe the tedium of teaching the same basic skills over and over again. It is this repetition of instruction that prompts many experienced teachers with a wealth of knowledge to seek other avenues outside the PE profession. Woods and Jeffrey (1996) write that teachers who fail to adapt to change experience stress and burn-out.

The creative agenda has much to offer in countering this scenario. The following section of this chapter looks at other ways in which we can offer valid and worthwhile physical experiences to our pupils. The list is by no means comprehensive. It is intended as an indicator of the range of activities that could be offered to pupils.

Ice hockey and ice skating

If your school is near an ice rink it may be possible to arrange for ice skating lessons and sessions. There are thirty-eight ice skating rinks in Britain, some of which are promoting links with schools in some way. For many of the rinks, ice hockey is a key part of their existence and they offer opportunities for children to join their junior clubs (see www.icehockeyuk.co.uk and www.iceskating.org.uk).

Tri-golf

Many schools are now offering their Year 5 and 6 pupils tri-golf as part of the PE curriculum. Sets of tri-golf clubs are available from most suppliers of PE equipment to schools. The equipment comprises bright yellow plastic clubs and putters together with dense sponge golf balls. The game can be taught on any open space but obviously playing fields offer the best option. Holes can be marked out using flat plastic hoops and the tees could be marked by numbered plastic discs. I ask the pupils to design a nine-hole golf course based on the space available, making use of any natural hazards. Once this is done the pupils can set the course out. They work in groups of four or six depending on the size of the class, each group starting at a different hole. They can play either as individuals or in pairs.

Secondary golf

If the playing fields are big enough it is quite possible to offer golf as part of the PE curriculum. Used golf clubs are often available either through the local golf club, Internet auction sites such as eBay, or advertisements in the local paper. Golf clubs and balls can be picked up at a surprisingly reasonable rate. It would not take too much imagination to set up a driving range with cones/flags to denote distances and targets. This, of course, would depend on the space available in order to ensure that risk assessment needs were met. As with several other sports, this activity may appeal to those pupils who prefer an individual sport requiring high levels of skill and application.

Mini squash

Mini squash is aimed at 5- to 11-year-olds and offers pupils an ideal introduction to the sport. There is much potential for the development of squash at the primary stage as part of the PE curriculum. The children really enjoy the game. The great advantage of any wall game is that pupils do not spend their time running after misplaced balls and the practice/playing time is therefore used very effectively. With some thought, initiative and ingenuity it is possible to find wall space and this activity could be part of a net/wall unit offered in the summer term. See www.minisquash.com for more information.

Cheerleading

This sport is not just for females and males can play their part in developing stunts that require or develop a great deal of upper body strength. The activity also encourages team building. When the group is building a stunt, the flier at the top has to be able to trust whoever is at the bottom. This is one of the fastest growing sports in the USA. It has great potential in terms of offering an activity that requires both males and females to work together to build routines. There are safety issues, however, and the work would need to be strictly supervised. Those schools that have adopted this as part of their PE curriculum have found it to be a very worthwhile activity. See the Future Cheer website for more information (www.futurecheer.net).

Pilates

Pilates can be complementary to traditional games because of its effects on core conditioning. Pilates can also help the growing number of school children who have neck and back problems caused by spending too many hours in front of a computer. It needs to be taught by a qualified instructor because of the specialist knowledge required (see www.pilates-institute.co.uk for further information).

Yoga

Yoga teaches body awareness and improves balance and coordination. It also enhances muscular strength, endurance and flexibility. There are yoga exercises that are specifically for children (Cheesbrough and Woodhouse 2006). Many teachers who have taught this to pupils have commented on how well the pupils have received it. They appreciate the physicality involved and clearly understand the focus and purpose of yoga. Teachers have often commented on how yoga calms the pupils down and allows them to succeed in a measured way without the stress involved in very active competitive situations. The teachers who have introduced it into the PE curriculum at both primary and secondary level have learnt their yoga through taking part in adult yoga classes. Some teachers have been so interested and inspired by the potential of yoga for young people that they have undertaken yoga courses in order to teach it to their pupils.

Games from around the world

I like to include a 'games from around the world' unit of work in my teaching. The purpose of this is to make pupils more aware of different cultures and their games and to see the commonalities we have with other cultures. It also allows the pupils to see that game-playing is something inherent in the human condition. Children in every culture play versions of tag games and ball games. In primary school this works well with a theme-based approach. There is no reason why this approach could not be used in the secondary PE curriculum with careful selection of the games. The best source of information is Kirchner's (2000) book *Children's Games from Around the World*.

Parkour

Parkour was developed by two French teenagers in a Parisian suburb from the 'parcours' or obstacle course of physical training used by the military. It focuses on uninterrupted, efficient forward motion over, under, around and through obstacles (both human-made and natural) in the environment. Such movement may involve running, jumping, climbing and more complex techniques. The aim of Parkour is to adapt one's movement to any given obstacle in one's path (see www.urbanfreeflow.com).

Young people see Parkour as a 'cool' sport and at least two secondary schools in London have sought to use its appeal to develop a more creative approach to PE lessons. The way to set it up in secondary schools would be to recreate in the sports hall or gymnasium the sort of urban settings the pupils may come across outside school. This could involve using boxes, wall-bars, beams, mats and benches. There are obvious safety concerns but if the pupils have had a thorough grounding in travelling, taking weight on their hands and jumping and landing in their gymnastics units of work they will be able to work safely in this environment. For streetwise young people this approach could make PE 'cool' and relevant to their lives. They would be able to create and develop new and exciting movements that would challenge and stretch their physical ability.

Ultimate Frisbee

Ultimate Frisbee is played between two teams of seven players on a large rectangular pitch. A line drawn across the pitch at either end creates two end zones (like American football). These are the goal-scoring areas. A goal is scored when a team completes a pass to a player standing (or more likely running) in the end zone they are attacking. (There are official measurements for the pitch and end zones, but in schools it is best to adapt this to the fitness levels and ability of the players.) Players cannot run with the frisbee (the players call it a disc rather than a frisbee). When they catch the disc they have to come to a standstill and throw it to another player, rather like netball. Also similar to netball, the players are allowed to pivot on one foot before passing. By passing from player to player the attacking team attempts to progress up the pitch towards the end zone. If the disc hits the floor or is intercepted or knocked down by the other team then the opposition takes possession. Possession also changes if a receiver is outside the playing area when he or she catches the disc. Ultimate Frisbee is essentially non-contact. Any contact between players can be declared a foul. The game is unique in that it is refereed by the players themselves, even at world championship level, according to a code of conduct known as 'the spirit of the game'. This places the responsibility for fair play on the players themselves. In this respect, playing Ultimate Frisbee is a completely different experience from playing other sports.

I have taught this in both primary and secondary schools and the pupils really enjoyed the challenge and exhilaration of the game. Most of them had some experience of throwing a frisbee but there was obviously a period of skill learning before the game could be played properly. It is a fast-flowing and very active game, which would be very suitable for developing tactical awareness and fitness levels.

Disc golf (frisbee golf)

Disc golf is a sport in which individual players throw a flying disc (frisbee) into a basket or sometimes at a target. As with golf, the object is to play a number of holes in the least possible throws. Most holes are a par three because of the need to fit a course into the space available. The 'hole' is a metal basket with chains hanging over it. However, for school use a post or target would do as well. This is a very worthwhile summer activity and those pupils who like individual sports rather than competitive team sports should really enjoy the challenge and skills involved.

Mini handball

Handball is played very widely in Europe and in many other countries. It is an integral part of the PE curriculum in many European countries and is an Olympic sport. It is an extremely enjoyable invasion game that combines the skills of throwing and catching a hand-sized ball with the fun of scoring by throwing the ball into a goal.

Both boys and girls play the mini handball game. There are four outfield players and one goalkeeper. For Key Stage 3, six-a-side would be fine. The teacher can determine the length of the game. During the game everyone in the team should take a turn in goal. The ball should be soft, not too heavy, must bounce well and should encourage a 'fear-free' game. The ball should have a circumference of 44–49 cm. This means it can be thrown and caught in one hand. The goal is shaped very much like a hockey goal, with a recommended 2.40×1.60 m dimension. There needs to be a goal area consisting of a semi-circle of 5 m radius from the middle of the goal.

Rules

- Players can move anywhere on the pitch except for the goal area.
- The goalkeeper may leave the goal area except when he or she has the ball in hand.
- Players are only allowed to hold the ball for 3 seconds.
- Players may move three paces with the ball.
- The ball can be played with the upper body but not the legs or feet.
- The ball can be bounced as often as desired.
- Players may hold the ball with both hands on two occasions, but not a third.
- Players are not allowed to hinder an opponent.
- If the ball goes out of play the other team throws it in again.
- If a player prevents an obvious chance of a goal, the opposing team are awarded a penalty shot.

Softball

Softball is a popular alternative to rounders. The larger softball bat and larger softball means that players have a much greater chance of making meaningful contact and hitting the ball greater distances than in rounders. A regular softball is, in fact, very hard and I would not like to recommend playing with this in curriculum time. There are a number of softer, safer alternatives available from sports suppliers.

The key to the game is to ensure that the fielding team have baseball gloves (these are available from most school sports suppliers. There is an initial outlay but the gloves do last and will provide a meaningful addition to the summer curriculum). The pupils enjoy the challenge of learning how to catch with the glove. For right-handed people the glove is worn on the left hand, leaving the right hand free to throw. Unlike rounders, the softball pitch is set out in a diamond shape. The bases can be purchased quite cheaply from school sports suppliers (go for the heavy-duty plastic bases, which will last a long time, rather than the official regulation ones). Most pupils have an idea of how the game is played, having seen it in movies and on television.

New-age kurling

This is an activity that the pupils will really enjoy. New-age kurling is a form of the original curling game but is adapted so that it can be played on any smooth, flat surface like a sports hall floor. One of its advantages is that it can be played equally well by both able-bodied and disabled people. The game is played with rubber curling stones and pushers. The stones have to stay in the vinyl curling-style target, which can be moved to an appropriate distance for the participants.

TOP Activity

This initiative, sponsored by Sainsbury's, offers alternative out-of-school hours activities for 7- to 11-year-olds. It is designed to reach those young people who might not be accessing physical activity through traditional routes. Although it is intended for out-of-hours activity, I think it has much to offer in terms of extending and developing choice within the PE curriculum. It could certainly be adopted for use at Key Stage 3 to reach those pupils who are not responding to the 'normal' PE activities on offer. It offers activities in four themes:

- Xpress yourself – dance, jive, salsa, cheerleading, martial fitness
- Xercise highs – skipping, hula, oppy relays, wake 'n' shake, circuits
- Xtra time – small side games, parachute
- Xtreme challenges – circus moves, tri-golf, rock-it-ball

Conclusion

There is no doubt that there are a great many effective and inspiring teachers of PE, both in primary and secondary schools. Many PE teachers have always been creative; they have had to be because of shortages of equipment and space. Some have been highly original in response to the type of pupils they teach. Creative teachers are able to see alternatives and continually evaluate the effectiveness of an approach they have undertaken. They have holistic perceptions and are able to perceive and meet the needs of pupils as individuals rather than just meeting the requirements of teaching a skill or a sport. They have the flair and ability to develop teaching ideas and innovations. They have the adaptability and flexibility to cope with changing circumstances.

The intention of this chapter has been to provide some examples of how the PE curriculum could be enhanced by the inclusion of activities not normally associated with the subject. Hopefully, pupils will both enjoy and learn from the opportunities provided by these different experiences. Lifelong physical activity encompasses a wide range of activities, many of which are not traditionally taught in the PE curriculum. With the worrying increase in childhood and adult obesity, the time is right for PE to play a key role in improving the long-term health and well-being of our children. By being creative in your PE lessons and curriculum, you can inspire pupils to undertake lifelong physical activity.

References

Cheesbrough, M. and Woodhouse, S. (2006) *Helping Children with Yoga*. London: Network Continuum Education.

DfES/DCMS (2002) *Learning through Physical Education and Sport: A Guide to the Physical Education, School Sport and Club Links Strategy*. London: Department for Education and Skills.

Jess, M. and Dewar, K. (2004) 'Basic Moves: Developing a Foundation for Lifelong Learning', *British Journal of Teaching PE*, 25(2): 23–27.

Kirchner, G. (2000) *Children's Games from Around the World*. Boston: Allyn and Bacon.

Lavin, J. (2001) *The Implementation of the National Curriculum for Physical Education*, unpublished PhD thesis. Manchester: University of Manchester.

QCA (1999) *Teaching, Speaking and Listening in Key Stages 1 and 2*. London: Qualifications and Curriculum Authority.

Thorpe, R., Bunker, D. and Almond, L. (1986) *Rethinking Games Teaching*. Loughborough: University of Technology.

Woods, P. and Jeffrey, B. (1996) *Teachable Moments: The Art of Creative Teaching in Primary Schools*. Buckingham: Open University Press.

Chapter 3

Teaching dance

A framework for creativity

Glenn Swindlehurst and Alison Chapman

Introduction

Dance is an important part of the physical, emotional and cultural development of every child. It features in all cultures as a social activity. It develops coordination and uses movement to communicate expression and historical concepts. The key fundamentals of movement taught in high-quality dance lessons develop a kinaesthetic awareness of movement at an early age and underpin movement in all later sporting activities.

What is dance and why teach it?

What is dance and why do so many teachers feel that they do not have the confidence and subject knowledge to teach it? For some teachers, even the word 'dance' can evoke powerful negative responses.

> What then is dance? It is one among many symbolic modes of communication by which everyone may formulate and express their understanding of the world, their way of life and each other.
>
> (Brinson 1991)

> Dance is a popular social activity, a prime means of expressing cultural heritage and identity, a dynamic and continually changing art. It is part of the cultural fabric of contemporary life.
>
> (Arts Council of Great Britain 1993: i)

The idea of communication is also one of the key skills identified in the National Curriculum. It talks about developing this skill through literacy, but dance and movement are also about communication.

The link between language and movement is fundamental and is expressed in many ways, such as 'jumping for joy', 'rushing around' and 'stamping in anger'. It is this communicative aspect of dance that can be the key to teaching creative dance.

DANCE AT KEY STAGE 2 (GLENN SWINDLEHURST)

Teaching dance in a primary school can be a stressful situation if you are a trainee or even an experienced class teacher, especially if you lack confidence or do not understand what to teach. Many primary teachers lack both the confidence and subject knowledge to teach dance. This has been evidenced by the demand for in-service training. Resources such as TOP Dance, developed by the Youth Sport Trust, have been requested nationally through the National Professional Development Programme.

A study involving trainee teachers' perceptions of teaching dance in primary schools by Rolfe and Chedzoy in 1997 revealed that there were a lot of inexperienced role models in schools that students might imitate. What emerged from student interviews 'was a low level of perceived teacher confidence and subject knowledge in teaching dance' (Rolfe and Chedzoy 1997: 226).

The development of dance in the curriculum

Over the last century dance has changed, from its focus on the physical fitness of children at the beginning of the twentieth century through to one of creativity and individual self-expression at the beginning of the twenty-first century.

Of course, children's physical fitness is still relevant today with the rising obesity problem and lack of physical activity among children. However, dance has much more to offer than just keeping children fit.

The purpose of this chapter is to promote the notion that creativity is the central, most important feature of dance. For many children dance can be the best way for them to communicate ideas and feelings. The process of creating a dance is a unique learning process that no other subject can provide.

The National Curriculum at Key Stage 2 asks that children should be taught to create and perform dances using a range of movement patterns, including those from different times, places and cultures. The range of possibilities offered by this is endless. However, there is one common characteristic: the creative process.

Dance and movement

Dance helps children to develop both locomotor movement skills, such as walking, running, hopping, jumping, skipping, galloping and travelling, and non-locomotor movement skills, such as balancing, twisting, stretching, turning and bending.

These activities help children to develop what is called the fundamentals of agility, balance and coordination. Dance can help develop the attributes of:

- Agility – in dance we might have sudden changes of level or direction, twisting and turning movements or different ways of travelling using the body.
- Balance – some movements in dance require a good level of symmetrical and asymmetrical balances.
- Coordination – travelling in different ways and using different body parts in different positions around the body and space.

Developing these attributes will not only help a child in dance, it can help them in all physical activities and sports.

The creative dance process

Laban's idea was that movement could be described under four headings:

- action (what is done by the body);
- dynamic (how the body moves);
- space (where the body moves); and
- relationship (who or what the body is moving).

Movement, therefore, can be simply defined as:

- *What can the body do?* Actions of locomotor and non-locomotor movement skills (i.e. running, jumping, skipping and stretching, balancing, etc.) using different body parts and body shapes.
- *How can the body move?* Quickly, slowly, strongly, lightly, etc.
- *Where in the space around you?* Up, down, forwards, backwards, sideways, left, right.
- *Who or what is the body moving in relation to?* A partner, a group, a prop.

(See Figure 3.1.)

Teachers who are not dance specialists can take Laban's principles and these questions as a starting point and use them as a framework to help children create dance sequences in school. The aim of creative dance is to develop children's movement through exploring and using their imagination, which will help develop some dance skills in performing, composing and appreciating. Ultimately, it is the process of educating the child through movement, not just the product of a created dance or dance performance. The process is as important as the product.

Example of the process using action words

There are five ways to move the whole body, or just parts of the body, in dance:

- travel;
- jump;
- turn;
- gesture; and
- stillness.

The first part of the process is to look at what the body can do:

- travel: running, crawling, creeping, sliding, shuffling;
- jump: hop, spring, soar, leap, bounce;
- turn: spin, twirl, whip, pivot, unwind, spiral;
- gesture: stamp, punch, wave, lean, reach; and
- stillness: wait, pause, freeze, suspend.

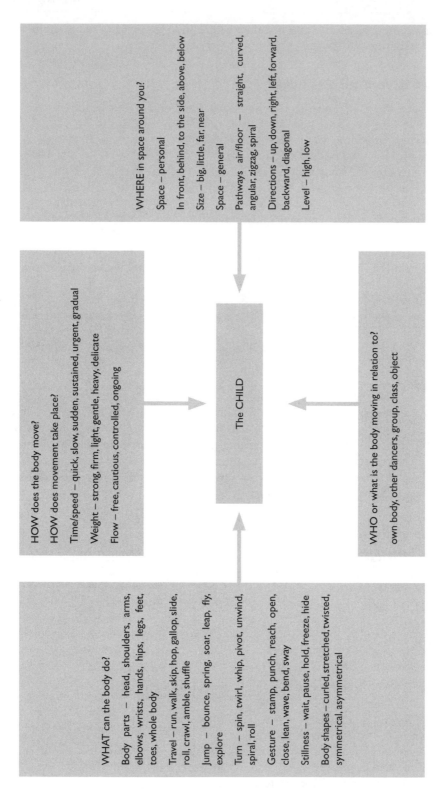

WHAT can the body do?

Body parts – head, shoulders, arms, elbows, wrists, hands, hips, legs, feet, toes, whole body

Travel – run, walk, skip, hop, gallop, slide, roll, crawl, amble, shuffle

Jump – bounce, spring, soar, leap, fly, explore

Turn – spin, twirl, whip, pivot, unwind, spiral, roll

Gesture – stamp, punch, reach, open, close, lean, wave, bend, sway

Stillness – wait, pause, hold, freeze, hide

Body shapes – curled, stretched, twisted, symmetrical, asymmetrical

HOW does the body move?
HOW does movement take place?

Time/speed – quick, slow, sudden, sustained, urgent, gradual

Weight – strong, firm, light, gentle, heavy, delicate

Flow – free, cautious, controlled, ongoing

WHERE in space around you?

Space – personal

In front, behind, to the side, above, below

Size – big, little, far, near

Space – general

Pathways air/floor – straight, curved, angular, zigzag, spiral

Directions – up, down, right, left, forward, backward, diagonal

Level – high, low

The CHILD

WHO or what is the body moving in relation to?
own body, other dancers, group, class, object

Figure 3.1 The creative dance process.

Here, action words have been used to help describe the movement. You will notice that some words can describe ways of moving that can be interpreted in more than one of the five ways. For example, hopping could be interpreted as travelling or jumping, and whip could be interpreted as turning or a gesture.

The action words are the method we use to begin creating a dance. Everyday movements can be described using Laban's headings of action, quality, space and relationship, which make it possible for everybody to create a dance through using descriptive action words.

Children may not fully understand how to perform the action word to really communicate the idea at first. Therefore, your role is to help children with the second part of the process, that is, how to perform the movement so they can improve the quality of their movement. There is a strong relationship between language and movement; one enriches the other and children do become interested in how words can describe their movement.

This is a list of action words. It is not a definitive list, but it provides basic descriptions of movement and stillness:

melt	fly	stay	slither	reach	hover	whirl	grab	linger	run
gather	creep	trot	dash	hold	gallop	jog	spin	kick	shake
bounce	wobble	walk	touch	explode	step	dab	scatter	unwind	twirl
curl	slip	settle	whip	hop	soar	stride	cascade	press	stop
hurl	punch	scurry	rest	zoom	tiptoe	swirl	freeze	spiral	stretch
shoot	pause	flounce	twist	roll	march	crawl	perch	slide	tilt
grow	shunt	bend	gyrate	wait	skate	spring	pounce	halt	float
unfold	tiptoe	skim	plunge	crumple					

For dance we need a stimulus. Almost anything can be used as a stimulus and can be divided into four main groups:

Auditory/aural	e.g. stories, poetry, music, natural sounds, percussion
Visual	e.g. pictures, photographs, objects, artefacts, colour
Tactile	e.g. sculptures, materials, objects such as coal, ice and fur
Environmental	e.g. seasons, animals, weather, natural forms

Example of a dance warm-up using action words

Ask the children to explore different ways of travelling using action words but focus on exaggerating their movement.

Use a DVD remote control as a tool. Each of the following buttons on the DVD remote control is assigned a specific movement:

Play	walking in space, keeping away from everyone else
Rewind	walking backwards carefully
Rewind low	can be done on all fours as a backward crawl
Stop	freeze the action the child is involved in
Record	copy your actions or those of the pupil whose name you call out

All these actions can be changed to fit in with the movements you want to revise, or through the use of 'Record' you can ask them to copy your movements or a style of movement that you are going to develop later in the lesson.

Ask the children to explore gestures such as a wave or showing anger. Focus on exaggerated gestures that communicate waving at someone you like and being angry with someone you don't. How do you use your body differently?

Ask the children to create a simple dance phrase using travel and gesture that uses exaggerated movements to reflect if they are happy or angry.

Action words to explore themes for dance

Identify a theme or topic; it may be one that you are already using in school. The following themes for dance are given as examples of developing approaches suitable for Key Stage 1 through to the top end of Key Stage 2. They are:

- Mr Men;
- bear hunt;
- Disney;
- winter;
- comic characters;
- sporting dance; and
- martial arts.

Use the following *process* as a way of planning movement ideas for dance:

- Choose a stimulus. This could be a poem, story, object, picture, etc.
- Explore the use of action words to explore stimulus, such as travel, turn, jump, gesture, stillness. Add music if applicable.
- Explore how to improve the performance of the action words.
- Select ways of combining action words into a dance phrase.
- Evaluate and improve dance phrase.
- Refine and practise dance phrase.
- Perform dance phrase.

Theme: Mr Men (exploring opposites in movement)

INTRODUCE THE IDEA

Use the Mr Men books to introduce the characters that the children will be using to explore different types of movement; for example, Mr Strong, Mr Jelly, Mr Rush, Mr Slow, Mr Quiet and Mr Noisy. Discuss strong, fast and slow characters. Read Mr Quiet and Mr Noisy to the children. Do they know anyone who is noisy or quiet?

MOVEMENT MATERIAL

Vocabulary/language: run, dart, wobble, shiver, shake, stamp, skip, fast, strong, statue, quick, slow, freeze, still, noisy, stamping, banging, silent, forwards, backwards, on the spot, sideways.

DANCE IDEAS/FRAMEWORK

1 Mr Strong – what actions can represent Mr Strong?
2 Mr Jelly – what actions can represent Mr Jelly?
3 Create a sequence of getting ready for school like Mr Strong.
4 Repeat the sequence but like Mr Jelly.
5 Consider the same sequence for Mr Rush and Mr Slow.
6 Ask the children to find a space and show a shape that looks as though they are going to move suddenly and very fast.
7 Ask the children to explore rushing actions in different pathways.
8 Instruct the children: 'on the spot in your own space show fast rushing movements'.
9 Link to Mr Rush activities from the book.
10 Remind the children of Mr Slow: 'show me how slowly you can travel'.
11 Ask the children to stand in a space and 'show me a shape which will tell me you are doing your slowest ever movement'.
12 Ask the children to do slow moves 'using your whole body in bends, stretches, twists and slow motion steps'.
13 Ask the children to create a dance, linking two fast moves and one slow move.
14 Work with a partner to put together a fast and slow dance.
15 Evaluate the dance.

The use of the voice is important when exploring action words and creating dance phrases. Through your expression, your voice can do the action that they are performing. If we use Mr Slow, you can draw out an action with your voice, such as 'walk v – e – r – y s – l – o – w – l – y' or 's – t – r – e – t – c – h up'.

Or when they are performing as Mr Rush: 'go, go, go, go, rush, rush, rush, be still'. These bursts should be short because they are intense. You could make links with knowledge and understanding of health and fitness by asking the children to explain the difference to their breathing when performing as Mr Rush and Mr Slow.

Theme: 'We're going on a bear hunt' (by Michael Rosen/Helen Oxenbury)

INTRODUCE THE IDEA

Describe/read the story and look at the pictures.

MOVEMENT MATERIAL

Vocabulary/language: swish, splash, splosh, squelch, stumble, trip, tiptoe.

POSSIBLE DANCE FRAMEWORK

1 Walking, chopping through the long grass – large, small steps, sweeping movements, pushing back the tall grass.
2 Paddling, swimming through the river – one foot in and quickly pulling it out again, gradually paddling and finally using swimming actions then shaking the water off at the other side.

3 Plodding and pulling feet through the mud – getting stuck (stillness) and jumping over puddles.
4 Shivering and shaking through the snowstorm – using different body parts, shivering and rubbing to get warm, being blown around, using turning actions.
5 Creeping and tiptoeing through the cave – moving quietly and carefully, freezing when you see the bear.

There could be linking phrases between each section where children march on the spot and use some words from the story.

Theme: The Jungle Book *(Disney DVD)*

INTRODUCE THE IDEA

Watch part of the DVD of *The Jungle Book* where they sing 'The Bare Necessities' and discuss the types of movements Baloo and Mowgli perform during the song.

MOVEMENT MATERIAL

Vocabulary/language: *clapping, elbow flapping, peeling, eating, rubbing, scratching, walking.*

DANCE IDEAS/FRAMEWORK

1 Walking on the spot getting the rhythm, walking in and out of each other getting the rhythm.
2 Shake arms like Baloo, combine walking with shaking of arms.
3 Clapping the rhythm of the music (at different levels, clap using different body parts).
4 Elbow flapping (on the spot, when moving).
5 Combination of above.
6 Peeling bananas.
7 Rubbing backs together as if scratching an itch.

PERFORMANCE IDEAS

Half of the class stand on a magic spot, the others walk in and out of them (in time with the music), swinging their arms or flapping their elbows or eating bananas. Change over. 'Next time as you reach another child rub backs with them. Change over'. Any combination of these ideas can be explored for a 'follow my leader' type of activity.

Disney DVDs are a great source of material for dance. The way characters move in the films and the expressions they show to communicate how they move and feel can help children with their performance.

Theme: winter

Consider the ideas linked to the theme:

snowflakes	Christmas	skiing	snowboarding	frost	cold
skating	icicles	warm clothes	snowmen	freezing/thawing	

Select an idea as a starting point: *freezing/thawing*

Select some appropriate action/movement words:

freeze	melt	drip	stiffen	prowl	stretch	flutter	whip	trace	creep
float	sparkle	fall	snap	drift	revolve	crackle	cascade	swirl	

Select at least one word for each of the basic actions as long as it is appropriate for the type of movement you are trying to communicate (Table 3.1).

Create a phrase of movement to include your chosen action words.

The idea of freezing and thawing is quite an abstract idea to put movement to and some teachers would really struggle with teaching that idea. Another teacher may choose skiing or snowboarding for example and come up with the action words: *fly, whirl, hold, spin, kick, whip, soar, zoom, fall, turn, twist, slide, zigzag, glide, dart, lean* (Table 3.2).

One movement phrase might be to start with stillness and in a ready position looking downhill, then travel in a zigzag pattern down the slope before zooming downhill, ready to jump and soar through the air, whipping round and making a 360° turn before landing, stopping and waving to the crowd. This would be *stillness, travel, travel, jump, turn, travel, gesture*.

Once you have a dance phrase, how do you make sure that it does not become like mime or drama?

Theme: comic characters

INTRODUCE THE IDEA

Show pictures and videos of different comic characters; for example, Homer Simpson, Bart Simpson, Dennis the Menace, Minnie the Minx, Desperate Dan, Spiderman, Horrid Henry, Disney characters, those in Harold Lloyd and Charlie Chaplin films, Monty Python, etc. Discuss how the characters move and what type of character they are.

Table 3.1 Action words winter theme: freezing/thawing

Travel	Jump	Turn	Gesture	Stillness
drift	sparkle	melt	swirl	freeze

Table 3.2 Action words winter theme: skiing/snowboarding

Travel	Jump	Turn	Gesture	Stillness
zigzag, zoom	soar	whip	wave	hold

Select some appropriate action/movement words:

creep	scurry	leap	dart	run	amble	hide	pounce	listen	slide
tiptoe	pull	push	turn	spin	throw	crawl	reach	turn	twist

Create a phrase of movement to include your chosen action words.

1 Give the children pictures of comic characters and ask them to choose one character. Ask them to create a simple dance phrase to communicate that comic character to include travel, turn, jump, gesture and stillness.
2 Ask the children to get into pairs with a partner who has a different cartoon character. In a pair, make up a story using both characters. For example, Homer and Dennis the Menace: 'Homer is asleep in the garden, Dennis creeps up and catapults him with a stone, Homer wakes up and chases him but stops at the doughnut shop'.
3 Ask the children to create a new routine to communicate their story and ask them to think about a clear starting and ending position.
4 Ask the children to evaluate their own performance and that of other pairs.
5 Ask the children to practise dance phrases again, taking on board any of the comments that could help improve the performance of the dance.

Perform the dance phrase.

This comic dance example can be adapted to meet the needs of children in different year groups, but fits in with the learning objectives of QCA Dance Unit 4.

In this unit children focus on creating characters and narrative through movement and gesture. They gain inspiration from a range of subjects, and work in pairs and small groups.

Theme: football

Any sporting movement can be used as a stimulus for dance. This example uses football. It is easy to get hold of video of football to explore the types of movements used. Football links easily with travel, turn, jump, gesture and stillness.

INTRODUCE THE IDEA

Use videos of football games, or pictures and football stories.

MOVEMENT MATERIAL

Vocabulary/language: *kick, pass, head, turn, jump, sprint, dodge, jog, spin, strike, step, tackle, shoot, stretch, soar, knee.*

DANCE IDEAS/FRAMEWORK

1 Warm-up exercises before kick off.
2 Ball skills (without a ball).

3 Tackling phrase, winning the ball in a header.
4 Kicking, travelling, dodging, passing sequence.
5 Travelling dribbling sequence leading to shooting.
6 Celebration phrase finish with a gesture.

The ball skills section might look at the tricks that can be done with the ball, such as keeping the ball in the air. Let the children identify with their favourite footballer. Using an imaginary ball, ask the children to flick it up on the right foot, then onto the knee, then the shoulder and then the head and back down the opposite shoulder, knee and foot. What would you look for in terms of quality of movement? Are their eyes on the ball? Does it look like they are controlling a ball or just going through the motions?

Remember this is dance and not drama. If you think about a kick, the quality is a strong striking leg action, which uses arms in opposition. This movement needs to be developed for dance purposes and made more abstract. To turn a kick into a dance movement it needs to be made more rhythmic and exaggerated.

The kick can be developed by:

• Exaggerating the size of the kicking action.
• Changing the level of the kick (kick off one knee or sliding kick).
• Changing the speed (slow it down as in an slow motion action replay).
• Changing the direction of the kick.
• Adding different actions before or after the kicking action such as a hop or a turn.

Examples of skills and footwork in football turned into dance phrases:

Kick – travel ⇒ kick at a high level ⇒ turn ⇒ travel ⇒ gesture
Head – travel ⇒ jump (head), turn ⇒ travel ⇒ kick ⇒ celebrate

What other ways could you devise of connecting movements using kicks, heading, celebrating?

Theme: martial arts, one-to-one combat

Martial arts are another stimulus that children enjoy. One of the main martial arts used in dance is Capoeira.

Capoeira is an art-form from Brazil, which blends elements of dance, music, rituals and fighting techniques. Brazilians call Capoeira a game; it is *played* not fought. Capoeira is believed to have been developed by slaves brought over from Africa to Brazil and while there is uncertainty about its origin, there is no doubt that dance and fighting techniques had a big part in its development.

There are three basic movements in Capoeira:

• the *ginga* – a three-step move;
• the negative and the role – forms of movement on the floor; and
• the *au* – a form of upside-down movement.

During the 1970s, Capoeira started to spread around the world, first introduced through dance shows and companies. Demonstrations by these dance companies are believed to have influenced the development of breakdancing.

One stimulus for introducing the theme of martial arts is computer games such as Tekken. In Tekken 3 and 4 there is a character that specialises in Capoeira and they also show different types of martial arts. This type of game uses a format of one-to-one combat.

INTRODUCE THE IDEA

Watch videos of children doing martial arts, such as karate, and look at the movements. What type of movements are they? Soft, hard or strong? Point out that the movements tend to be asymmetrical and have angles.

Discuss what those who practise martial arts (such as judo, karate, taekwondo) do before they train or fight. Why do you think they do that?

MOVEMENT MATERIAL

Vocabulary/language: *kick, punch, explode, grab, spring, knee, step, press, stance, pause, spin, halt, open, close, stand, hit, rise, roll, freeze.*

DANCE IDEAS/FRAMEWORK

1 Before combat: stillness, gesture (respect). Circling opponent; small, whole body actions; individual body part actions showing different fighting postures.
2 Combat: one-to-one combat (no contact) action and reaction to hitting and being hit; change between quick and sudden and slow and controlled actions.
3 The finish: the finishing blow and celebration, but showing respect to opponent.

DEVELOPMENT OF THE THEME

1 Ask the children to show a position (i.e. stance, punch or kick) of someone doing martial arts in a frozen position. Emphasise strength and angularity.
2 Pick out good examples emphasising strong postures and angles.
3 Ask the children to try a position someone else has done.
4 Ask the children to perform a small jump in the air before freezing in one of the positions. Next, try a jump, and punch or kick in the air before landing.
5 Ask the children to run before jumping and kicking in the air.
6 Discuss the ritualistic greeting before two martial artists fight and explore different examples of this sign of respect.
7 Ask the children to create a dance phrase before the combat begins; for example, greet, run, jump with punch, freeze in fighting posture, circle opponent, run, jump with kick, freeze in fighting posture, lower to ground and roll into another fighting posture. Circle opponent.
8 Evaluate performances. Are there examples of strength in frozen positions and angles in the shapes?

9 The dance phrase uses travel, jump, stillness, travel, jump, stillness, travel (a turn could be added while travelling). What action words could be used and how should the body move? In this dance they also need to think about where they both move in relation to each other.

Dance frameworks

All teachers have the ability to improve how children move and the qualities of their movement through observing how they interpret the action words and giving feedback on how to improve the qualities of weight, flow, speed and time.

Smith-Autard (2002) explains that primary teachers working with action words and creating dance phrases need to learn how to make what the children create more dance-like. The main answer lies in *stylisation* rather than *technical* refinement. To achieve technical refinement in any skill takes a long time of continued practice. The easiest way to achieve stylisation is through exaggeration of the movement. Giving actions a rhythmic pattern can also make the movements more dance-like: 'Stylisation, then, can be achieved through exaggeration, elaboration and rhythmic structuring of the everyday action' (Smith-Autard 2002).

What we have looked at is creating very simple dance phrases, and the development of these phrases to create a dance framework. These frameworks can come from a theme the children are working on in the curriculum, including music, stories, poems and objects.

Dance is an effective and integral part of the whole curriculum. It can be part of any cross-curricular topic work, so that aspects of a topic may be learned through movement.

USING PROFESSIONAL DANCE WORKS TO TEACH DANCE AT KEY STAGE 3 (ALISON CHAPMAN)

Earlier in this chapter, ideas of how to instil an enthusiasm for dance at an early age were encountered. If children receive a strong grounding in this field at primary school, it is important that dance at secondary school continues to build on those creative experiences. Whatever their primary school experience, the early years at secondary school will greatly influence the enjoyment that children will gain from dance and from expressing themselves creatively through movement.

In the last five years the number of pupils choosing to study dance at Key Stage 4 and beyond has rapidly increased. It is vital that dance education in schools is of a high enough quality to adequately prepare pupils for further study. An important point was raised by Smith-Autard (2002), who indicated that schools that have been successful at teaching dance at GCSE and A level 'have no choice but to go beyond the syllabus indicated in the Physical Education National Curriculum for England Order of 2000'.

The aim of this section is to show how dance is vital in fulfilling the PE Key Stage 3 National Curriculum and how, by using creative approaches, you can expand the ideas and ways pupils express themselves through dance and deliver high-quality dance education that will help them appreciate different dance styles and prepare them for further study.

If asked what value dance has in the National Curriculum, PE teachers will commonly answer that it fulfils the creative aspect of learning composition, easily allows pupils to film their performances and therefore access the use of ICT, and allows them to evaluate their own performance. Such comments indicate that dance is an activity that is sometimes undervalued and underused in schools.

The main focus of this chapter will be to give a rationale for how teachers can use professional dance works to provide a framework for studying dance. It will show how professional dance can unlock creativity in the child and contribute to high-quality PE lessons, which will engage youngsters in dance and provide them with an enriched cultural experience at the same time.

Dance and the Key Stage 3 Programme of Study

The Physical Education Programme of Study for Key Stage 3 (QCA 2007) is centred on providing high-quality provision that will enable pupils to develop performance, analytical and evaluative skills and the confidence to participate in a range of activities which contribute to a healthy lifestyle. Dance is an activity that can meet much of the National Curriculum's intention to develop balanced, physically educated youngsters.

If dance is to be used to meet many of the National Curriculum criteria, some thought must be given as to how it can contribute to the four key concepts.

1 Competence

In dance pupils perform whole body skills, such as leaps, turns and balances, and they develop fine manipulation skills in the use of gestures and body isolations. They develop compositional skills in a range of dance styles and the ability to choreograph solo and group dances. They study movement in a range of dance styles; for example, contemporary technique or street dance.

2 Performance

Pupils gain knowledge of how to hold posture and project movements in a performance situation. They learn to evaluate performance and what needs to be done to improve the expression and quality of movement portrayed to the audience. They work collaboratively and sensitively with others to ensure safe execution of movements and correct timing with others in the dance.

3 Creativity

Pupils find imaginative ways of using the body and manipulating movement to communicate a theme or idea through dance. They explore through improvisation and then adapt and refine the techniques in composition to express ideas.

4 Healthy, active lifestyles

Pupils should enjoy participating in a range of dance styles, including aerobics, jazz and contemporary, and use the fundamental movements that underpin the techniques to improve physical fitness. They learn about safe exercises to ensure that participation is not dangerous and they learn about social dancing to enhance physical and mental well-being.

Being creative through dance

Creative dance, more commonly known as modern educational dance, has been around since the 1940s, when Laban (1948) suggested that the emphasis of dance should be on the process of dancing and creating dance; the release of emotions; enjoyment; the expression of feelings; and use of imagination – and that these were more important than the actual product. The current National Curriculum has introduced a more balanced approach in which the process is important but also levels of skills are emphasised. It is also generally recognised that knowledge of choreography and expression of creativity should be evident in the finished product, which would provide a basis for assessment. As teachers, it is not our job to give pupils all the answers, but to ensure pupils have the tools to explore movement, ideas and expression in a creative way so they can find their own response to a range of tasks.

An advantage of dance is that everyone can achieve and be successful at some level. Whatever their ability all pupils can have success in dance even when they have little success in other activities. For example, a child with poor hand–eye coordination may rarely hit the tennis ball with the racket, but in dance such children can use their bodies in many ways to express themselves successfully. When composing a dance, children can extend their skills by selecting movements they can perform well and therefore achieve success. For some children, the prescriptive actions, skills and techniques required in performing some sports might prevent them from being good performers. They may not have developed the skills needed or may lack the necessary abilities that underpin those movements.

However, in dance all children have the opportunity to express themselves sensitively. If children have limited success in an activity, it is not likely that they will enjoy themselves or choose to participate in that activity later in life. In dance at Key Stage 3 there are no set movements that the child is required to perform for assessment. It is good practice for teachers to provide movement phrases to copy in order to increase the skill level or provide a starting point for a creative task, but movement phrases are easily differentiated and adapted to select appropriate movement material for different pupils.

Using professional dance performances as a framework to study dance at Key Stage 3

When asked what they find the most difficult activity to teach, a large proportion of PE teachers will answer 'dance'. Among the reasons for this is a lack of personal experience when they were themselves pupils at school, and a lack of training and ability to demonstrate movement with good posture and quality.

Teachers often feel that lack of training and ideas for units of work reduce their confidence to teach dance. They do not always have innovative ideas to choreograph their own movement phrases or produce movement to challenge the most gifted pupils in their lessons. If we the teachers are not creative or confident in our approach, it is difficult to unlock the creative potential of others and ensure that our pupils are confident to explore expression through movement. Similarly, if pupils are influenced by ideas solely from their PE teacher, it is possible that some will not receive culturally diverse dance opportunities. This section will provide examples of how professional dance can be used in lessons to meet the requirements of the Key Stage 3 National Curriculum to improve the skills of pupils and encourage them to be creative in responding to tasks.

Many schools host professional dancers or companies to deliver dance workshops or hold dance festival days where professionals work with pupils in a number of ways. They may teach a technique class to improve posture and the actions pupils can perform, or deliver a creative workshop where pupils learn a small movement phrase often taken from the professional's current repertoire. The pupils may then use their own creative ideas to adapt and choreograph a dance from the original movement material. If the company is performing locally the pupils may then get the opportunity to see the dance performance live. Such opportunities are excellent and enrich the development of the pupils. They can often prove to be a memorable and inspiring experience for children. However, they can also be expensive and are often not developed further.

By using recorded dance performances the work is sustainable and all pupils in the year group can have a similar experience. The recording can provide the foundation for a unit of work where movement material is used as a stimulus for developing creativity. It can help pupils to use imagination to compose a dance that communicates a theme; increases their skill level; shows a distinct dance style and compares different pieces of dance. A recording may also be used to demonstrate the different ways choreographers put movement together, and the relationships between dancers, space and dynamics.

Currently, if pupils elect to study dance at GCSE, BTEC, A level or above, they are required to study, and have an appreciation of, professional dance works. In order to make lessons interesting and to increase the understanding of the pieces, teachers have created lessons that involve the study of set dance works in a practical situation. Rickett-Young's (1997) book for GCSE dance students refers to the use of existing recordings of dance to teach dance effectively. Dance teachers with training in dance will have experienced the use of professional dance as a stimulus and starting point for creative projects. This is not an approach widely used by many PE teachers, who are often not dance specialists, and so have not been exposed to the variety of performances available.

Sometimes pupils who have enjoyed their early dance lessons in school elect to study it at GCSE level or above but then find it very difficult to bridge the gap and work to the required level. This is often because of a lack of experience of professional dances and their lack of exposure to abstract themes for composition. Introducing a professional resource-based teaching approach in Key Stage 3 would not only prepare them for further study but also educate them in dance appreciation and give them a greater understanding of dance and choreographic styles, and confidence to build their own. The resource-based approach also gives non-specialist dance teachers examples of movement material to use in lessons that may improve their own confidence and enable them to explore a wider range of teaching styles.

Many dance practitioners advocate this approach to teaching dance. Smith-Autard (2002) asserts that 'pupils learn as much about the discipline through the study of professional ready-mades as they do through responding to the tasks within the bounds of their own imaginations'. Rolfe and Harlow (1997) focused a whole book on ways to use professional dance in lessons and suggested that 'it is by developing aesthetic awareness and artistic understanding of given dance works that children and teachers can enhance their own creativity in dance'.

Part of the National Curriculum involves the study and understanding of a range of dance styles. An effective way of achieving this would be to show video footage of professional dance, which allows pupils to gain a full understanding of the style and the costumes involved. For example, seeing a small excerpt showing some of the key components of Indian dance would be more effective than a teacher describing and demonstrating them. Rolfe and Harlow (1997) support this use of video recordings of dance: 'every child has the opportunity to access dance from diverse cultures and artistic traditions, including a range of dance styles'.

The increase of technology in schools and the secondary strategy of developing ICT across the curriculum (ICTAC) mean that the use of video/DVD recordings of dance should be accessible to most PE departments. One of the main advantages of having a recording of dance is that it can be replayed many times if required to learn a section. Also, snippets of dance can be found and played to meet the needs of the lesson. The use of pre-recorded dance in lessons will provide opportunities for pupils to:

- develop an appreciation of different dance styles;
- observe some professional dance, which they may not have the opportunity to see outside school;
- enhance and extend their own performance;
- extend the range of movements they can perform;
- increase the vocabulary of movements they use in their own choreography;
- engage with interesting visual stimuli;
- have clear demonstrations to aspire to;
- use some of the movements or gestures as a starting point to create their own dances;
- use a theme from a dance and then respond imaginatively with their own ideas to communicate the theme;
- develop an understanding of choreographical techniques by seeing them in action and then applying them to creating their own dances; and
- improve evaluation and interpretation skills and to develop a deeper understanding that may be applied to their own work.

A few guidelines to help you use recorded dance effectively

- Decide the purpose for using the recording; for example, is it to copy a section, as a stimulus for a theme or to highlight a choreographic device?
- Do your research, name the dance and the choreographer and have an idea of what the dance is about – the pupils are bound to ask questions.

- Ensure you know how to use the ICT equipment and check that it works prior to the lesson.
- Ensure the video is at the right place prior to the lesson or you know exactly the minute at which it appears on the DVD.
- Show small snippets of dance – for Key Stage 3 do not spend all lesson watching a dance. Select the small sections that highlight the purpose. Do not show more than 10 minutes as pupils may get bored or lose focus. Small sections of about 2 to 3 minutes' length are ideal.
- If copying a section, make sure you have planned and rehearsed this yourself prior to the lesson. It is not advisable to play a video for pupils to copy themselves – this will only waste lesson time as they may copy it incorrectly or even back-to-front. Also, you may need to stress safe methods if learning more challenging movements.
- You may want to show several different extracts if you want to show a range of dance styles or possibly choreographic ideas, for example the use of canon and unison.
- Give pupils the opportunity to see the extract again.
- Give pupils the opportunity to see the whole dance in their own time if they are particularly interested.

Rolfe and Harlow (1997) advised that 'the viewing of dance should be devised to inform children's understanding through attending to objective features in the work . . . [and provide] . . . opportunities for children to respond intuitively to what they see and feel through exercising their imagination'.

Professional dance and the National Curriculum

This section will focus on some of the ways in which professional dance may be used to meet the requirements of the National Curriculum, with a more detailed focus on the aspects that are new to the Key Stage 3 Programme of Study 2007.

Figure 3.2 provides some ideas for activities and outcomes that demonstrate how the use of professional dance works could be used to fulfil the criteria set out in the Key Stage 3 Programme of Study.

In order for you to plan effective schemes of work to address the Key Stage 3 Programme of Study there follows some guidance on what dance works are available and which aspect of dance the recording would be suitable for. Table 3.3 provides an overview of the key processes and lists some resources you may wish to use to teach that aspect of the National Curriculum.

The following section provides examples of further detailed activities and tasks that may be used in lessons to develop performance skills, compositional knowledge, the range of roles pupils can experience and cross-curricular projects against the relevant paragraphs contained in the Key Stage 3 Programme of Study 2007.

Roles

Pupils take on a range of roles:

Leader – to teach others movements or warm-ups

Performer – performing dance or set phrases

Choreographer – composing a dance

Director – observing and staging a dance

Critic – evaluating and interpreting a dance

Performing

Copy set phrases from the piece to develop technical skills.

Observe the performance to develop an understanding of performance skills.

Teach an excerpt to develop an understanding of the qualities of different dance styles.

Compare own performance to further develop evaluation skills.

Evaluating and improving

Observe professional, own and others' work to describe the actions, evaluate strengths and weaknesses in both performance and choreographical form.

Suggest appropriate ways to improve the dance and or performance.

Analyse and interpret the meanings of dance and evaluate the effectiveness at communicating the theme.

Ideas of how to use professional dance performances to teach KS3 dance

Composing

Develop an understanding of how to create a dance from an idea or stimulus.

Use improvisation to gather suitable movement material and select and refine material to communicate the emotion or theme.

Apply a range of choreographical principles to compose a dance and explore relationships, time, space and dynamics.

Dance appreciation

Understand some of the differences between dance styles, e.g. ballet and contemporary techniques.

Understand the history and roots of different dance styles e.g. Indian dance compared with street dance.

Understand how set/stage and accompaniment can impact on a dance.

Understand the difference between dance as a social activity and for a purpose and art form.

Healthy lifestyles

Use professional dance techniques and safe practice of warm-up and cool-down in lessons.

Develop key components of fitness as seen in videos, e.g. flexibility and strength.

Use dance and aerobics as a method of developing stamina.

Use dance as fun and developing social well-being, e.g. salsa and ballroom dances.

Develop an enjoyment of dance for pupils to enjoy outside lessons, e.g. street dance.

Cross-curricular links

Some professional performances have stimuli or messages linked to other National Curriculum subjects, e.g. science or geography.

Observe different dances and then explore how they communicate the theme through movement, e.g. use of abstraction and gesture.

Use of dynamics to show an emotion.

Use of space, pathways and formations to give an idea, e.g. conflict could show 2 v 3.

Figure 3.2 An overview of activities that could be used to fulfil the KS3 Programme of Study.

Table 3.3 Examples of professional dance works suitable for teaching KS3 Dance

Aspect of KS3 Programme of Study	Examples of professional dance works
2.1 Developing skills in physical activity a. refine and adapt skills into techniques develop the range of skills they use develop the precision, control and fluency of skills	*Swan Lake* by Matthew Bourne *Still Life at the Penguin Café* by David Bintley *Swansong* by Christopher Bruce *Ghost Dances* by Christopher Bruce *Beginners Salsa* by Orod Ohanian and Dessy Ohanian *Dance, Dance Wherever You May Be: An Introduction to Indian Dance* by Sanjeevini Dutta and Sarker Bisakha *West Side Story* by Jerome Robbins *Making of Maps* by Shobana Jeyasingh
2.2 Making and applying decisions Select and use compositional ideas effectively in different creative contexts Refine and adapt ideas and plans in response to changing circumstances Plan and implement what needs practising to be more effective in performance	*Swan Lake* by Matthew Bourne *Still Life at the Penguin Café* by David Bintley *Swansong* by Christopher Bruce *Ghost Dances* by Christopher Bruce *West Side Story* by Jerome Robbins *Nutcracker* by Matthew Bourne *Troy Game* by Robert North *Singini in the Rain* by Gene Kelly and Santley Donan (director) *Rooster* by Christopher Bruce *Cross Channel* by Lea Anderson *Making of Maps* by Shobana Jeyasingh
2.3 Developing physical and mental capacity Develop their physical strength, stamina, speed and flexibility Develop their mental determination to succeed	Any professional dance that is physically demanding and gets heart rate up above 60% maximum heart rate or requires performers to improve fitness components to sustain performance. *Swan Lake* by Matthew Bourne *Still Life at The Penguin Café* by David Bintley – 'Southern Cape Zebra', 'Hognosed Skunk Flea' and 'Texan Kangaroo Rat' sections. *Swansong* by Christopher Bruce – prisoner solo sections *Ghost Dances* by Christopher Bruce – opening 'Ghost' section Aerobics and pilates videos/DVDs

QCA Programme of Study Key Stage 3

Paragraph 2.1: Developing skills in physical activity

a Refine and adapt skills into techniques.
c Develop the precision, control and fluency of their skills:

  • Copy set sequences from the professional piece.
  • Replicate movements from the professional piece.
  • Copy phrases from performances in varying dance styles.
  • Record performance of the dance to inform how to improve.
  • Perform to an audience within the group or to an external audience.

These activities, for example, could be the starting point of a unit of work. Pupils should watch the section they are to copy a few times on video or DVD. This creates a mental image of what they are aiming to achieve. A key phrase could be copied with the aim of increasing the number and range of movements they can perform, performing movements in a particular style or contrasting styles, or forming the basis of a creative task. Selecting a phrase that involves a range of fine, gross and contrasting actions will help develop their coordination and possibly have an impact on fitness components such as flexibility.

Performing the sequence in front of others encourages a sense of performance, projection and quality of movement.

Paragraph 2.2: Making and applying decisions

a Select and use compositional ideas effectively in creative contexts.
b Refine and adapt ideas and plans in response to changing circumstances.
c Plan and implement what needs practising to be more effective in performance.
d Recognise hazards and make decisions about how to control any risks to themselves and others:

- Use the professional dance as a starting point. Show the pupils small sections so they can appreciate the style, theme or use of a choreographical principle.
- Pupils learn a small phrase from the professional dance; they can then explore different ways of putting those movements together without adding any extra movements. This can be done using choreographical devices such as repetition, change of action, body part, speed, space and direction.
- Pupils observe a section of a dance and select the key aspects of style, theme, dynamics or motif.
- After observing, the pupils select four movements from the professional dance – for example, gestures, movements or motif – and link them together and add some movement material of their own choice in the same style. This is a very good activity that allows for pupils' own creativity and also differentiated work as the pupils select their own movements that challenge each of them as an individual. An extension activity would be where the pupils teach each other the phrase they have choreographed.
- Pupils choreograph a dance in the style of a chosen professional piece.
- When pupils have choreographed a phrase of movement they then experiment by varying the use of space, dynamics and time to communicate the theme of the dance.
- Pupils may select their own theme but use a choreographical idea from a professional dance work to help communicate the theme and vary the relationships within the dance using mirroring, matching, canon and unison.
- Once you have initially taught some safe lifting and supporting techniques, the pupils may use a range of support techniques as appropriate, even copy some lifts, balances or holds from the professional dance and then add the movement to their own dance. This will involve some aspects of risk assessment, pupils (with guidance from you) being able to recognise movements appropriate to their level of ability. It will also involve safe lifting and supporting techniques.

- In groups, allow pupils to video and observe a performance of their choreography and evaluate its effectiveness. Pupils should learn to evaluate the compositional elements of the dance and how effective the piece is in communicating the theme of the dance. They should then be allowed time to adapt, refine and improve the piece before a final performance in front of an audience.

It is beneficial to use some aspects from professional dance in order to stimulate the pupil's creativity. Some pupils are able to create from nothing; others need ideas and a stimulus to help give them ideas to get started. Some of the activities listed above give a good basis from which to be creative. Smith-Autard (2002) is in support of using dance recordings to help with the creative process to ensure all pupils learn and achieve: 'Given total freedom, without such vocabulary, students of this age in particular will freeze and produce nothing.'

These activities will help to develop an understanding of how to manipulate, change and put together movement to form movement phrases. The pupils will also explore using time, weight, space and flow in their composition. This will help their kinaesthetic awareness of how changes in those aspects can give a different expression and visual effect to the dance. Pupils will have a greater understanding of the movements that form the basis of specific dance styles. For example, strong sharp movements are often found in street dance and these kinds of movements are good for communicating conflict. Slower, lighter movements with gestures would give a different expression.

By watching dances that show a range of groupings, such as individual, pairs, trios and larger groups, the pupils can be creative in the way they use relationships. They gain understanding that the performers do not all have to be in unison all the time but can use contrast to add interest to the dance. In exploring the use of relationships, pupils often show the most imagination in creating dance. They usually enjoy working in groups, as the movement possibilities are endless, especially when they start to develop support and lifting techniques.

Paragraph 4: Curriculum opportunities

b Experience a range of roles within a physical activity.
c Specialise in specific activities and roles.

Traditionally in PE, the various roles that pupils take on have been focused in Key Stage 4 where accreditations have been available and pupils have been encouraged to take on the roles of performer, official, leader and choreographer. In recent years there has been an increase in the number of leadership accreditations available to pupils and so the number of pupils taking on a range of roles in PE has also increased. As similar schemes, such as play leader, are available to pupils in primary schools, it is good to see that these roles are also becoming an important aspect of the Key Stage 3 curriculum.

Dance is becoming an increasingly popular activity with a range of opportunities for pupils to develop specialist areas. From age 14 pupils can now study for a dance leader's award. There is the need to develop a range of skills in dance that will complement that of other sporting activities. As professional dance companies usually have people employed in a range of roles to ensure their company runs smoothly, it would be a good start for pupils to take on similar roles.

PERFORMER

Pupils will dance, rehearse and perform for an audience, developing their skill level, quality of performance and ability to project to an audience.

CHOREOGRAPHER

The pupil creates a dance and makes the creative decisions about the intentions and movement of the piece and spends time working with the performers to ensure that they are all clear and able to perform the movements intended in the dance.

LEADER

The pupil organises a section of the lesson or dance and has the opportunity to teach others a dance routine or a warm-up.

DIRECTOR

This is the person who observes a dance and decides what changes need to be made in order for it to look good enough to perform in front of an audience. The decisions often involve changes to the spacing or staging of the dance and feedback to dancers on their performance. For example, the timing may need improving or dancers may need to change their angle to give the best view of the dance to the audience. This role is not creative and the director should not change the dance without the choreographer's permission.

CRITIC

This person will look at a dance and comment on the choreography, performance and communication of the theme. It is usually a person who sees the dance for the first time and so can comment on how effective it is and whether the dance and performance were effective.

CAMERA OPERATOR

This person records the dance for video/DVD. This person should have a good knowledge of the key parts of the dance and know when the cues are in order to zoom in or focus on the most important parts of the dance.

MUSIC OPERATOR

This is the person who operates the music as required. This person would have a sound knowledge of the starting and finishing positions of the dance and would be able to take cues from the dances and fade the music.

MUSIC/FILM EDITOR

As technology improves, dance is becoming more imaginative and choreographers both young and old often want to merge music. This person cuts and prepares the required accompaniment. They might also edit the recording of the dance to produce a DVD.

Extracurricular clubs might provide the opportunity for some pupils to extend any of these roles in producing shows for an audience outside of lesson times.

Paragraph 4: Curriculum opportunities

g Make links between PE and other subject areas of the curriculum.

With the further development of sports colleges, and case studies that show the positive impact that using sport and physical activity linked with other subjects can have on attainment levels, it is important that cross-curricular links are made with dance. Table 3.4 shows some examples of professional dance performances that have some links with other subjects.

It is important that cross-curricular links between dance and other subjects often developed at Key Stage 2 continue into the secondary school context, either by using professional dance works (as seen in Tables 3.3 and 3.4) or by using themes that have another link. Some dance projects may involve using the cross-curricular idea as a starting point to stimulate creativity and the product may not be true to the original theme. A preferred method would be to use the cross-curricular idea as the main theme running through the project, for example, a dance on the states of matter would involve the pupils learning about the properties of a solid, liquid and gas and then planning how they would translate this information into movement. Pupils would explore movement ideas, relationships between dancers and the use of space, time and flow to choreograph a dance that clearly communicates the theme to an audience.

Examples of themes that have a cross-curricular link and could be used for dance:

- states of matter (solid, liquid and gas), linked to science;
- the life cycle, linked to science;
- a study of speeds and forces, linked to science;
- a poem from an English lesson;
- study of Shakespeare (see Table 3.2 for details);
- shapes from maths, used as a stimulus to form a study on shape. Ideas could be spatial pathways on the floor and in the air, using symmetrical and asymmetrical shapes, complementing and contrasting shapes, lines and curves;
- erosion of the environment, linked to geography;
- global warming, linked to geography;
- the shapes of buildings, linked to design technology, art or geography;
- a historical study of dance, researching the history of dance techniques and producing a dance that has aspects of a range of dance styles or eras;
- a study of traditional dances from countries around the world as a link to modern foreign languages;
- a study of religious dance, for example Indian dance and dance for rituals, as a link to religious education;

Table 3.4 How professional dance can meet the requirements of curriculum opportunities

Curriculum opportunity	Application of dance
a. Get involved in a broad range of different activities that in combination develop the whole body	Use a range of dance genres which involve coordinating different body parts and dynamic use of the body, e.g. contemporary, ballroom, street dance, African dance
b. Experience a range of roles	As discussed above – leader, performer, choreographer, director, audience, critic, rehearsal director, music and camera director
c. Specialise in specific activities and roles	An extension of above maybe in extracurricular opportunities, e.g. teaching dance to younger pupils
d. Follow pathways in and beyond school	Take part in lessons, school clubs, out of school clubs, community dance groups, leading younger performers, involved in school and community shows
e. Perform as an individual, in a group or as part of a team in formal competitions or performances to audiences beyond classes	Take work from lessons or dance clubs and perform in assemblies or dance shows, for community, primary schools etc.
f. Use ICT as an aid to improving performance and tracking progress	Using video/DVD footage in lessons. Ensure pupils can use the video and music equipment themselves. Use video cameras to record pupils' own work and use in order to develop analysis and evaluation skills. Use playback technology to observe performance straight after the event. Some technology such as Kandle, Dartfish and DVDs can compare two performances so pupils can watch their own performance of a set phrase next to that of the professional dancer. Use dance made for camera, e.g. Cross Channel, and then set tasks for pupils to choreograph sections of dance specifically for camera, e.g. use of above filming, close-ups, zooming in and out. A project could involve making their own dance DVD using the work in dance lessons and then editing and producing the DVD in ICT lessons.
g. Make links between PE and other subjects and areas of the curriculum	Some professional dance pieces are made specifically for use in an educational setting and often have accompanying resource packs and CDs with frameworks to use in lessons. Often these resources have a cross-curricular theme as they are aware of how to use dance in a cross-curricular way. Examples of dance made for educational purpose are: *Perfecting Eugene* by Ludus Dance, based on science and the topic of genetics *Zygote* by Ludus Dance, based on growing up, relationships and pregnancy *The Making of Maps* by Shobana Jeyasingh, based on the medieval Mappa Mundi linked to cultural and spiritual concerns of life *Still Life at the Penguin Café* by David Bintley, based on extinction *Ghost Dances* by Christopher Bruce, based on folk dance and historical influences of South America It is possible to have any idea and produce a cross-curricular dance project. An example would to link art, history and geography by studying the artist L. S. Lowry and then producing a dance from the stimulus. *A Simple Man* by Gillian Lynne and performed by Northern Ballet is based on his life. An English project could be to take *Romeo and Juliet* and watch the characterisation into dance using one of the many dance interpretations available and then take on the role of critic and write an essay comparing the dance interpretation and the book.

- famous paintings or sculptures, used as a stimulus to creating a dance (see Table 3.4 for a professional dance-based idea); and
- creating music specifically for dance in music lessons and then choreographing a dance to that piece of music.

In conclusion, the movement and theme possibilities for enabling pupils to be creative in dance are endless. It is important to use dance as a tool to teach the whole child rather than focus purely on the activity. This way the child will have an enriched education, greater understanding of their own feelings and the confidence to express themselves through movement. The use of professional dance works is an effective way of unlocking the door to that creativity and skill.

Bibliography

ACE (1996) *Consultative Paper for Education and Training in the English Art Funding System*. London: Arts Council of England.

Arts Council of Great Britain (1993) *Dance in Schools*. London: Arts Council of Great Britain.

Ashley, L. (2002) *Essential Guide to Dance*. Second Edition. London: Hodder & Stoughton Educational.

Brinson, P. (1991) *Dance as Education*. London: Falmer Press.

Laban, R. (1948) *Modern Educational Dance*. London: Macdonald and Evans.

QCA (2007) *Curriculum Review, Physical Education*. London: Qualifications and Curriculum Authority (available at www.qca.org.uk/curriculum).

QCA (2007) *Schemes of Work*. London: Qualifications and Curriculum Authority (available at www.standards.gov.uk/schemes3/).

Rickett-Young, L. (1997) *Dance Sense Theory and Practice for GCSE Dance Students*. Plymouth: Northcote House Publishers Ltd.

Rolfe, L. and Chedzoy, S. (1997) 'Student Teachers' Perception of Teaching Dance in Primary School', *European Journal of Physical Education*, 2: 218–227.

Rolfe, L. and Harlow, M. (1997) *Let's Look at Dance!* London: David Fulton Publishers.

Smith-Autard, J. (1996) *Dance Composition*. London: A&C Black.

Smith-Autard, J. (2002) *The Art of Dance in Education. Second Edition*. London: A&C Black.

Most of the dance video/DVD resources mentioned are available from either Dance Books Ltd (www.dancebooks.co.uk) or the National Resource Centre For Dance (www.surrey.ac.uk/NRCD).

Chapter 4

Creativity and gymnastics

Lawry Price

Values and principles

Gymnastic activities support the individual child's learning in becoming more confident, more skilled, more controlled and more precise in their physical movement capabilities.

If children's creativity is to be extended by the provision of support for their curiosity, exploration and play, they need to be provided with opportunities to explore and share their thoughts, ideas and feelings – movement activity, and the provision of gymnastic activity, is a perfect medium through which these objectives can be achieved.

This chapter looks at how teachers might facilitate creativity for their children and pupils through gymnastic activities. First, we will examine the significance of learning opportunity in this area, and move on to examine what needs to be in place to ensure that the creative instincts of children can be supported and given rein in this important aspect of their PE.

What does a PE curriculum look like without a gymnastic activities element? What do children in the 7–14 age group potentially miss out on if they are not provided with learning opportunities in this particular area? Why might it be considered detrimental to children's well-being, their general health and their overall physical development if at least in each year of this growth period an exposure to refining basic movement competency is not visited? Why, in essence, is gymnastics a fundamental part of the PE curriculum? How is it a unique experience in its own right for its participants?

This sample of set questions, and their implications, recognise not only the importance of enabling children, at a vital stage of their development, to learn about how their own unique bodies move, but also how to use it to confront and succeed with the ever-demanding challenges that the subject area of PE potentially provides. As part of their professional ethics, teachers hold to a premise that each and every child they teach is unique, and therefore seek to facilitate their learning needs accordingly. It follows that all avenues of possible provision should be sought to maximise on the personalised individual abilities that all growing children have.

If an area of learning can provide cognitive, affective and *physical* benefits then it supports a notion that this is a worthwhile, meaningful, appropriate and relevant experience, worth pursuing and of value to its participants. That this might be achieved through an exposure to what some physical educationists might see as the essence of their subject – *gymnastic activity* – then a further case can begin to be made for its contribution to children's creative abilities too. There is little debate that the basic physical skill competencies that children need to master in their formative years are encapsulated within well-designed, continuous, progressive units of work to which gymnastics can contribute significantly. The control, coordination and discipline to be learnt from full engagement in gymnastic activity provides the basis from which all other areas of movement development draw, including the very important elements to daily life of locomotive, general stability and manipulative skills.

Can we add to this impressive list of benefits *creativity*? In this particular gymnastics-focused context, creativity can be interpreted as giving licence to children's individual bent for putting an individual stamp on the work they produce, their own unique interpretation in meeting the demands of a particular task, their own response to using the skills at their disposal to producing a performance that their own body enables them to perform. This is, after all, what we expect to see when we observe and appreciate the very top gymnast at international and elite level – individuality and uniqueness of performance. With a teaching approach employed that both facilitates and allows for such outcomes, the area of gymnastics learning can be transformed into one of major benefit for all its prospective participants within this age group, with transferable skills and understanding accruing along the way.

To ensure that this laudable objective can be achieved, a set of key markers for you to adhere to in your quest to provide the quality of learning experience and successful outcomes you desire from your gymnastics teaching might look like the following:

1 Plan units of work thoroughly, with associated focused themes and individual lesson activities, that are informed by the stage of development at which children within the classes are currently taught.
2 Retain consistently high expectations of what children are capable of, and be cognizant of the fact that they are enthusiastic and receptive to the gymnastic content presented to them, and at the same time bring their own ideas with them.
3 Be prepared to repeat and consolidate previous work in a variety of different ways and by applying alternative teaching styles and approaches to enrich the quality of work that emerges.
4 Present different and alternative tasks for floorwork that will lead to apparatus interpretation of the skills and the challenges that working at different levels poses.
5 Keep work levels high, fully participatory and with minimised instruction punctuating the flow of work produced.
6 Create positive learning atmospheres and environments by adopting and implementing consistent working routines, which need to be taught, learnt and applied – *they don't just happen!*
7 Maintain and continuously assess performance against stated criteria to inform ongoing planning and to maintain motivation and enthusiasm among the learners.

It is worth recounting here, as a postscript, that it is only through providing opportunities to learn, practise and thereby accrue experience that children's performances will improve and move forward in terms of quality. The same applies to one's own teaching – the more we teach in the area of gymnastics the more our own performance becomes more finely tuned and ultimately increasingly effective. This takes time but can only happen if we confront the challenge that gymnastics presents us with. For teachers this means accepting that we are learners within this process too. For children, the other learners in this process, we need to ensure we facilitate their right to move with increasing confidence, skill, control and precision and hopefully give them a forum for expressing their individuality, flair and personal interpretation.

Developing a rationale for gymnastics teaching

We cannot dismiss the fact that the teaching of gymnastic activities at primary level poses a particular set of challenges to the average primary school practitioner. A lack of subject knowledge may be at the heart of this but on a purely practical level coping with the demands of a class of 30 children of varied movement ability working in free space and potentially on apparatus of various size, shape, height and dimension adds to the dilemma of ensuring and maximising learning opportunities in this curriculum area.

This set of dilemmas can and does continue into secondary schooling, where evidence would suggest that similar issues exist with regard to teacher confidence levels, knowledge and expertise in teaching gymnastics. Indeed, the lack of reference in consecutive Ofsted reports to gymnastics teaching indicates that the amount of teaching that is going on in this area is on the decline. This may be traced back to the ITT syllabus or might reflect a more diverse PE curriculum that is now in play. What cannot be dismissed is the learning opportunities that are potentially missed if this provision is not available at a point where prior knowledge and experience stands to be more fully utilised and exploited by more fully developed and stronger bodies ready to take on more testing challenges.

The moment to revisit and restate the importance of the place of gymnastics in a growing child's education is opportune. The primary school has long been recognised as the place where the individual child's 'whole education' is looked after, where teachers value the opportunity to see advances in the full range of educational experiences and activities, and to witness the significant strides made during the period in both intellectual and physical capabilities. Gymnastic activity, as a fundamental part of the primary PE curriculum, has traditionally been the area of the curriculum where physical and therefore movement capabilities can be closely monitored and witnessed. It is the area where children can learn about how their bodies move, what different body parts can do in cooperation with other parts, and how those same bodies can move in space and in relation to other children sharing the same space. It is also the place where the challenges of working at different speeds, heights and levels, and following different routes and pathways, as well as coming into contact with a range of different surfaces, significantly occur.

In addition to this impressive array of potential physical learning benefits, the contribution that work in the area makes to learning in other PE areas, like dance and games, is an added consideration to be kept in mind when justifying the importance of gymnastics activities. The development of a particular movement vocabulary (Box 4.1) that promotes, for example, a variety of responses to ways of travelling, using space, making different body shapes, balancing on different body parts, jumping and landing

Box 4.1 Basic movement vocabulary for primary gymnastic activities

Gymnastic activity themes	Skills	Body	Spatial	Dynamics	Apparatus	Relationships	Movement skill vocabulary
Space	*Stability*	*Whole body*	*Personal*	*Speed*	*Portable*	*Individual*	On to
Use of apparatus	Balance	Large parts	Near	Go and stop	Mini apparatus		Off
Movement tasks	Stillness	Small parts	Next to	Fast	Hoops	*Partner*	Across
Supporting body weight	Dynamic	Fixed	Far away	Slow	Cones		Between
Lifting parts high	Inverted	Free	In front	Quicker	Skipping ropes	*Groups*	Up
Travelling	On different body parts	Near	Behind	Accelerate	Bean bags		Down
Feet together and apart		Far	At the side	Decelerate	Skittles	*Class*	Over/under
Curling and stretching	*Locomotion*	Leading	Following	Slower	Canes		Around
Use of space	Walking	Following	Leading	Short time	Discs	Work alone	Next to
Transferring weight	Jogging	Isolated		Long time	Mats	Work with others	Far away from
Joining movements	Skipping		*General*	Sudden	Benches	Copy	Through
Directions	Galloping	*Surface*	Directions	Stillness	Linking planks	Contrast	Underneath
Parts together and apart	Running	Front	Forwards		Nesting tables	Mirror/match	Into
Lifting and lowering	Jumping	Back	Backwards	*Weight*	A frames	Support actions	Out of
Shape	Rolling	Side	Sideways	Strong	Ladders	Talk and discuss movement	Near to
Speed	On different parts	Top	Diagonal	Powerful	Movement tables		Towards
Twisting and turning	Continuous	Bottom	Up/down	Firm	Boxes		Away from
Sequences	Paused	Shape		Light	Stools		Height
Levels		Arrow	*Levels*	Soft	Foam equipment		Length
Partner work	*Manipulative*	Ball	High	Tension			Width
Flight	Grasp	Wall	Low		*Fixed*		Obstacle
Pathways	Grip	Twist	Medium	*Time*	Frames		
Symmetry and asymmetry	Hook	Gesture	Near floor/surface	At same time	Ropes		
Balance and continuity	Hang		Away from floor/surface	Within a set time	Beams		
Flow	Spring	*Size*		After another	Bars		
Strength and lightness	Push	Big		Before another	Poles		
	Pull	Small		Use same space			
	Slide	Medium					

skills and working at different speeds, is very clearly required in the performance aspects of those core PE areas too. Your awareness of the potential for transferability of skill learning will enhance the overall knowledge, skills and understanding referenced as National Curriculum requirements. It could also be added that as children do acquire greater control, accuracy and versatility in their motor competence, so gymnastics can also bring a discipline to their motor performance, essential for the performance aspects of the work ultimately produced.

A rationale for teaching gymnastics in school settings could therefore be summarised as follows (see Figure 4.1 for an alternative formulation):

- *Why?* To service the need for children to become increasingly controlled and skilful in their physical movements and competences. Gymnastics in the school setting is primarily concerned with both gross and fine motor development and contributes markedly to gradual and progressive improvement in coordination, balance, flexibility, strength and stamina (specifically improving cardiovascular efficiency).
- *What?* To broaden and extend the repertoire of children's abilities in jumping and landing skills, rolling actions and taking weight on different body parts, and to promote a range of different travelling actions.
- *Where?* The ability to display the broadening range of skills on the floor, initially on simple apparatus constructs, and increasingly on the varied surfaces offered by a full provision of gymnastic apparatus, including apparatus that provides opportunities to work on various levels and at increased heights.
- *How?* Through a full range of teaching methods and an approach that promotes children succeeding at their own level – using teaching methods that focus on promoting the individual child's learning and success in physical activity.
- *When?* Consistently through well-thought-through, planned units of work over concentrated periods of time, consolidating what has gone before and extending the children's repertoire of skilful body actions.

To reiterate a point made earlier with increased justification with this rationale now fully stated, what would be the result of children not experiencing this area of learning? It might be appropriate to suggest if this was the case then a vital cog in children's all-round development would be missing, and there would inevitably be a shortfall in their physical performance capabilities. Furthermore, the wider brief of PE should not be understated. The subject generally, and gymnastics specifically, makes a major contribution to speaking and listening skills, children's aesthetic and artistic development and their ability to develop problem-solving skills, as well as nurturing interpersonal and observational skills. These are all invaluable life skills and part and parcel of the wider curriculum (Figure 4.1).

National Curriculum physical education – gymnastic activities

Gymnastic activities feature prominently in PE National Curriculum documentation (DfEE 1999) as an earmarked area of activity and learning that promotes knowledge, skills and understanding. The importance of PE is hallmarked in NC documentation by the statement that the subject '*promotes physical skilfulness, physical development*

WHAT? What body parts will be used, what actions, what shapes?

Whole body actions

Travel

Stillness/pause/balance

Rotate/twist/turn

Jump/spring/land

Curl and stretch

Body parts

Parts high/low

Balance on points/patches

Different parts leading

Relationship between parts

Open/closed/contact

HOW? At what speed, with what power and force, with what flow?

Dynamics of weight/speed/direction

Speed

Fast/slow

Sudden/patterned

Accelerate/decelerate

Stillness

Rhythm

Weight

Heavy/light

Strong/gentle

Pathway

Direct/forward/backward/diagonal

Flexible/curved

Flow

WHO? Will the movements be done individually, with a partner, as part of a group?

Individually

Individually within a group

With a partner/group

Meeting and parting

Mirroring

Matching

Leading and following

Contrasting

Rotating turns

Canon/performing together at the same time

WHERE? In which direction, at what level, following what pathways?

Personal space

In front/behind/to side

Above/below/diagonal

General space

Forwards/backwards

Sideways/diagonal

Up/down

Shape

Curled/stretched/twisted

Long/wide

Level

On the floor

High/medium/low

On the apparatus

Figure 4.1 Understanding gymnastic activity – analysis and development.

and a knowledge of the body in action'. There are also references to where this all begins within The Early Years Foundation Stage Statutory Framework (DfES 2007), where it is stated that by the end of the period children should *'move with confidence, imagination and in safety . . . move with control and coordination . . . travel around, under, over and through balancing and climbing equipment . . . show awareness of space, of themselves and of others'*.

This represents a clear reference to how gymnastic activities particularly are servicing the needs of children in promotion of these aims from the outset of their experiences in this area. Using these benchmarks as the building blocks on which to build children's further physical development, the *Physical Education in the National Curriculum* (DfEE 1999) documentation states that:

At Key Stage 1 in gymnastic activities pupils should be taught to:

a perform basic skills in travelling, being still, finding space and using it safely, both on the floor and using apparatus
b develop the range of their skills and actions (for example, balancing, taking off and landing, turning and rolling)
c choose and link skills and actions in short movement phrases
d create and perform short, linked sequences that show a clear beginning, middle and end and have contrasts in direction, level and speed.

At Key Stage 2 in gymnastic activities pupils should be taught to:

a create and perform fluent sequences on the floor and using apparatus
b include variations in level, speed and direction in their sequences.

When we look at the level descriptors for meeting PE attainment targets, it is clear where the referencing to learning within gymnastic activities appears within the statements. For example, at level 1:

Pupils copy, repeat and explore simple skills and actions with basic control and coordination . . . they start to link these skills and actions in ways that suit the activities . . . they describe and comment on their own and others' actions . . . they talk about how to exercise safely, and how their bodies feel during an activity.

At level 2:

pupils explore simple skills . . . they copy, remember, repeat and explore simple actions with control and coordination . . . they vary skills, actions and ideas and link these in ways that suit the activities . . . they talk about differences between their own and others' performance and suggest improvement . . . they understand how to exercise safely, and describe how their bodies feel during different activities.

At Key Stage 2, level 3 descriptors state that:

pupils select and use skills, actions and ideas appropriately, applying them with coordination and control . . . they show that they understand tactics and composition by starting to vary how they respond . . . they can see how their work is similar to and different from others' work, and use this understanding to improve their own performance . . . they give reasons why warming up before an activity is important, and why physical activity is good for their health.

At level 4, the culmination of where the work in all children's PE in primary schools should reach, the descriptors state that:

pupils link skills, techniques and ideas and apply them accurately and appropriately . . . their performance shows precision, control and fluency, and that they understand tactics and composition . . . they compare and comment on skills, techniques and ideas used in their own and others' work, and use this understanding to improve their performance . . . they explain and apply basic safety principles in preparing for exercise . . . they describe what effects exercise has on their bodies, and how it is valuable to their fitness and health.

The next stage, secondary school gymnastics, will see children working towards attainment targets at levels 5 and 6. The work and progress expected at 11+ will clearly be determined by what has happened previously. The demands of Key Stage 3 will ask of pupils to be able to:

a create and perform complex sequences on the floor and using apparatus;
b use techniques and movement combinations in different gymnastic styles; and
c use compositional principles when designing their sequences (for example, changes in level, speed, direction, and relationships with apparatus and partners).

At Key Stage 3, level 5 descriptors state that:

pupils select and combine their skills, techniques and ideas and apply them accurately and appropriately, consistently showing precision, control and fluency . . . when performing, they draw on what they know about strategy, tactics and composition . . . they analyze and comment on skills and techniques and how these are applied in their own and others' work . . . they modify and refine skills and techniques to improve their performance.

At level 6:

pupils select and combine skills, techniques and ideas . . . they apply them in ways that suit the activity with consistent precision, control and fluency . . . when planning their own and others' work, they draw on what they know about strategy, tactics and composition in response to changing circumstances, and what they know about their own and others' strengths and weaknesses . . . they analyze and comment on how skills, techniques and ideas have been used in their own and others' work, and on compositional and other aspects of performance, and suggest ways to improve.

The key note here for teachers teaching at primary level will be to bear this in mind when planning an appropriate gymnastics curriculum for pupils in readiness for the demands that pupils will face when entering secondary education (Box 4.2). The child that leaves their primary school with confidence in their movement abilities, and has at their disposal sound stability, locomotor and manipulative skills, will prosper from the typical PE curriculum to be offered at 11+. Gymnastics programmes in primary schools that have ensured this have done the job.

Box 4.2 Progression in gymnastics – Key Stage 2/Key Stage 3

KS2 – Children should be taught to improve their knowledge, skills and understanding in gymnastics by:	KS3 – Children should be taught to improve their knowledge, skills and understanding in gymnastics by:
• developing and using a range of gymnastic skills both on the floor and using apparatus; • performing sequences with greater accuracy and fluency on the floor and using a range of challenging apparatus; • designing sequences which make use of planned variations in speed, level and direction; • using compositional principles to adapt and develop sequences individually, with partners and in a group; and • describing how well a sequence is formed, evaluating it and suggesting ways to improve its design, fluency and accuracy.	• refining and adapting complex combinations of skills and agilities on the floor and using apparatus; • developing specific techniques in a range of gymnastic forms and styles; • designing, refining and adapting movement combinations into complex sequences using compositional principles; • modifying and developing their sequences for improved performance; • being clear about what they want to achieve in their work; • taking the initiative to analyse their own and others' work; • using the information to improve the quality (composition and precision) of their performances.

Of course, there will be children in every class who exceed these expectations and others who are still working towards the attainment levels set out in the documentation. What is crucial is for teachers to recognise the important role that gymnastics plays in pursuing an individual response to movement tasks set, and also to have and maintain reasonable expectations of children's abilities to respond naturally and within their capabilities. Gymnastic activities provide good evidence that children have reached milestones in their physical development – providing further challenge to both check and extend their performance levels is the role the teacher needs to play to service these objectives.

Teaching strategies for gymnastic activities – help and hindrances to progressive learning

As a starting premise, teachers who work with the youngest of children acknowledge that children are naturally inclined to be active and, if they are provided with the right type of opportunity and encouragement along the way, will physically develop naturally, and pick up much incidental learning as part of the whole process. If adequate time, space and apparatus are provided for gymnastic work, children will develop their skill, confidence and versatility just by being given such opportunities. If there also exists an emphasis on allowing children to make their own discoveries as to what their bodies can do, they will acquire knowledge about their capabilities, and progress will be marked by increased confidence, greater skill competence and more creativity in their movement during this phase of development. The skill of the teacher is to build on this natural development by giving direction and encouragement to get the children to think imaginatively about their movements. The bottom line is that the role of the teacher is all-important in developing the work – you can either assist progress or stand in its way.

The individual child, not just those who excel, is the focus of work in this area of the curriculum, therefore:

- Ensure the aims, intended learning outcomes and the theme of each lesson is clear – do not try to cover too much in one session. It is better to consolidate the learning with substance (and detail when applicable) than try to cover too much ground too quickly.
- Do not get in the way of the children practising and developing their ideas by too much teacher intervention – however great the temptation.
- Too little intervention, on the other hand, allows bad habits to develop and does not facilitate the correction of such faults – where intervention is concerned, a careful balance is needed.
- Do not expect the same response from all the children to set tasks – allow for individual interpretation, ideas of their own to flourish and their own creativity to influence what they produce, and acknowledge individual ability within groups and classes taught.
- Too much, or too little, emphasis on activity rather than quality in the work can be a hindrance – the balance has to be right!

If we want children to make the expected progress in this area of the curriculum then the following need to be implemented:

- Thoughtful, considered, consistent and careful planning, preparation and organisation.
- Vitality and enthusiasm generated by you, which spurs on a keen class and pro-motes a likewise response from children of all abilities and levels of interest and enthusiasm.
- Control and discipline within lessons, but this should not detract from positive, working atmospheres that are conducive to learning.
- A sound knowledge of movement principles, including how children move charac-teristically at 5 years as opposed to their abilities at 8 years and then 11+.
- Plenty of opportunity to allow classes to explore and make choices about their movement, to make mistakes that can be corrected through practice and further experimentation.
- Injection of praise, encouragement and support – the children will respond to commentary and feedback that show an interest in their work.
- Built-in opportunities to enable children to reflect on their work, to share their ideas with others, and to understand why the work is relevant, what is good work and why, and a recognition of quality in work observed.
- Highlighting of achievement – build on success for future reference.

First gymnastics lessons with new classes

The nature of teaching primary-aged children brings with it the challenge of meeting a different set of children each year. This clearly operates in secondary school provision too, albeit with many different classes across year groups as opposed to teaching one class the whole curriculum. This means that the need to inculcate children into the frameworks for delivery that match your individual knowledge, expertise and ways of doing things that work for you is always high on the agenda in September and October of each new school year. This is where gymnastics teaching and learning can greatly assist you in establishing empathy and class bonding, so crucial if expectations for the year are to have a good lift-off. The early observation of children moving in space, among each other, confronting the challenges of apparatus work, not least in the setting up and dismantling and putting away of the equipment, can tell you a lot about the strategies that will or will not work with your new charges. The knock-on effect to classroom practice will also benefit relationships and the early establishment of a rapport conducive to maximising the learning potential of the class generally.

A good way to address these concerns is to pitch a teaching unit of gymnastic activities at the very start of a new year, with some very general activity sessions to give you insight as to what needs to be covered and from what starting base. The first two lessons of the year with a new class could focus, therefore, on floorwork, followed by another on simple apparatus set-ups, possibly with another on a more complex format. The information enabling the planning of future input should emerge from this and also give a general picture of individual ability in the movement context.

Demonstration

Although there is no compulsion to use teacher demonstration to show children the skills, actions and movements we want them to master, there is little doubt that this helps in modelling the basics of good performance. There are alternatives – the particularly able child performer, the *best* attempt at the action demo, and so on. There is little to be gained by demonstration of a skill, an action or a movement that is beyond the capabilities of the vast majority of the class – demonstration can be off-putting if the skill is too difficult or too easy. The challenge must suggest that there is a quality to be aimed for that is attainable through practice and over time *by all*. It is far better that when presenting material to children you acknowledge that you are learning too. This puts all involved in the learning process on an equal footing, it will ensure that progression is in keeping with the abilities of the class, and in children's eyes it shows that teachers too are continuing their education at the same time as them! A lot of credibility can be acquired with such an approach and will further develop the relationship aspects that can be accrued in this area of the curriculum.

Progression

If real progress is to be achieved then individual planning should set out key learning objectives, with attainable assessment criteria that match, to ensure that learning is continuous and progressive. It also clearly needs to match children's capabilities, therefore prompting the need for regular and ongoing recording of children's achievement and attainment. The recognition that progress is only apparent over a period of time, not necessarily from lesson to lesson, is vitally important in this respect. Box 4.3 shows key markers for you to use when assessing progress over time. These are

Box 4.3 Assessing progress in gymnastics – twenty key markers

1   Changing for PE – Because children are motivated and looking forward to their gymnastics lessons they remember, with less reminding needed, to bring their kit, they change increasingly quickly for lessons and afterwards, and there is less fuss and bother with this important feature of PE generally. Children are more concerned with the content of the lesson to follow and with what they might achieve within its content, and look forward to the next lesson as a result of their experiences.

2   Beginnings of lessons and free choice issues – Children enter working spaces and have initial tasks to work on immediately. They also display greater independence of thought and action and increasingly creative ideas when presented with open-ended choices and tasks.

3   Assembling apparatus – The children become much more adept in carrying and assembling apparatus, and they do this increasingly speedily and efficiently and with increasing awareness of safety issues. They also display new ideas and creative thinking when given the choice to construct apparatus pathways.

4   Learning atmospheres – These become progressively more about quiet, controlled and concentrated work as children become increasingly immersed in and motivated by the work that is set. The 'sound' of a gymnastics lesson is concerned with moving bodies in space, and safe, controlled and resilient contact with the different surfaces offered by apparatus. Talk that does occur is focused on the work being produced and is recognised as contributory to the learning that is happening.

5   Use of space available – Children's awareness of the space available, floor and apparatus, becomes increasingly marked in terms of how they use it personally and in sharing and collaboration with others.

6   Grouping arrangements – Children learn to work in changing groups, are aware of moving around apparatus stations en masse, and can interpret different apparatus layouts according to tasks set. From early experiences of being part of a set group, they are able to cope with working with different children on a regular basis and share with them their ideas, understanding and awareness of safe work, including the erection and dismantling of the full range of apparatus available.

7   Impact work – This becomes increasingly controlled and resilient and always safe. Eye–foot coordination is at the core of more skilful work, with lightness and 'feel' increasingly to the fore.

8   Sustained performance – As energy levels and personal strength increase, children are able to work for longer periods, and can apply greater effort levels to their work. They are constantly 'on the lookout' for places to work, be it on the floor, apparatus or combinations of both; there is a quick start to practice and work; and by seeking out different starting and exit points there is a declining need to queue, particularly with regard to apparatus usage.

9   Whole body emphasis – As awareness grows of how the body and its constituent parts move, a greater range of combined actions are used with an emphasis on using the whole body. Agility and athleticism improve as mobility and increased suppleness become more evident. Extension and tension in body movement and action are increasingly a feature of the work produced, enhancing quality elements and adding to criteria for potential assessment.

10   Creativity and variety – The work produced displays an all-round improvement in quality as children add changes of direction and speed, work at different levels, follow pathways in their movement that are varied, and show differing body shapes in their actions. The continuity and flow of movement reflects the growth in ideas and the individuality to be promoted in response to tasks set and themes being explored.

11 Understanding and knowledge – As experience, and therefore knowledge, develops, the application of previous learning comes increasingly into play as different themes, tasks and activities are presented in the work.

12 Confidence and self-esteem – Best witnessed with children's ability to work at different heights, when the body is upside down, and in skilfully working in close proximity to others. As children become more aware of their capabilities they are increasingly prepared to confront more challenging tasks and confront these with personal drive and determination in order to succeed, ever mindful and conscious of ensuring safety principles in their work.

13 Performance skill – Individual skill thresholds rise so that more difficult and challenging tasks and more complex series of actions can be achieved. An example would be the ability to perform a head-stand with legs extended and held for a slow count of three, and to be able to come out of that immediately into a forward roll to a controlled finish.

14 More precise and defined work – With younger children the work will emphasise a highly individualised, experimental, free choice set of characteristics. As children become more skilled they will be able to respond to tighter, more defined tasks, and work towards more exact and accurate performance, drawing on the repertoire of learnt skills and techniques accrued over time.

15 Body control – Improvement of flow of movement and the ability to exert the right level of muscle tension in a variety of situations is exhibited. General 'body management' is enhanced – children are more in control of their bodies.

16 Collaboration and cooperation – The ability to work as an individual, with a partner, or in groups, sharing ideas and learning from others, reflects a growth of social skills to be promoted in gymnastics. The sharing of workspace, and the need for cooperation when assembling apparatus, are two clear examples where this is evidenced, but so is the ability of children to be increasingly able to adapt and share their own ideas when working with others.

17 Movement flow – The ability to devise more complex sequences of movement, and to link actions ever more smoothly, is a developmental characteristic of gymnastics work.

18 Quality work – Emphasising the need to plan, practise and modify initial ideas links thought and action requirements. Adding personal style and gloss (or 'flair') is an important part of working towards making the final product – the performance – real quality work.

19 Children's attitudes – Gymnastic activities provide opportunities to develop body skill and therefore confidence and enhanced self-esteem in children. This can be carried over into other learning situations and be exploited further in other curriculum areas. The enthusiasm, willingness to 'have a go', pride in showing good work, and confidence accrued over time from success in this area are the hallmarks of a well-motivated child.

20 Key skills enhancement – Children's key (or core) skills of stability, locomotion and manipulation are greatly enhanced by a continuous, progressive gymnastic programme. There should be discernible progress made in all these areas as children become the more skilled, more competent, motor-efficient beings we expect them to be by the time they leave the primary school in readiness for the more defined PE curriculum of the secondary school.

Adapted from *Primary School Gymnastics* (Price 2003).

particularly focused on children's performance in a wide-ranging array of features that give clear indications of learning progress *in* and *through* gymnastics.

Children tend to produce what is expected of them and you need to ensure they have a clear picture of what can be achieved in gymnastics over time. The setting of high standards, and the demand for children to produce their best efforts at all times, help the individual child develop as a person as well as someone who is becoming *physically educated.*

Links with other work

Cross-curricular perspectives are an essential consideration when you are planning for gymnastics teaching. However, this should not be tokenistic, contrived or artificially construed. The language elements are crucial to delivery, for example action words that can evoke movement response, naming of body parts, what apparatus is properly called, and how we can design interesting apparatus layouts to suit skills development. Bringing learning accrued from other curriculum areas to life is where gymnastics can score heavily in developing and widening knowledge and understanding initially (but not always) gleaned elsewhere. For example, the words *sequencing* and *symmetry,* which will have emerged in mathematics work, will have a different meaning when applied to movement, particularly in a gymnastic sense. Your ability to respond to such possibilities in your teaching maximises the effectiveness of cross-curricular approaches and such an approach acknowledges your own skill in educating the whole child – an opportunity not to be missed.

In essence there exist plenty of opportunities to bring together work in the class-room with the work to be covered in gymnastics and PE lessons as a whole. Whether it be through use of music, or elements of drama that act as a stimulus for work, or a simple child self-assessment of performance through picture and word format, the possibilities are endless. Consolidation of knowledge and understanding should be at the forefront of thinking and delivery here, utilising the concept of educating the 'whole' child through different means. That action and movement take place, and are immediately evident to the observer, makes this area of the curriculum significantly distinct and therefore flexible in the way learning takes place – a benefit to reap for many other subject areas, not just in the primary curriculum but also within the defined subject curriculum at Key Stage 3.

Extracurricular work – the school gym club

Where possible, such provision should be available to all children who have an interest in developing further the work that is covered in normal lessons. How far the work can be extended will very much be dictated by the knowledge base and expertise of the teachers prepared to make such provision. If the teacher has been the recipient of further training and personal coaching in the area then the possibilities are potentially marked. On the other hand, extracurricular opportunities for children can be provided by motivated (and enthused!) teachers at any practioner level who wish to offer extra provision to move individuals' learning and performance levels forward. This is very much the case at primary level and is practice to be commended. That it might also lead to further training, as part of ongoing professional development, can only be of benefit in the long term.

An important consideration when providing these opportunities is to be consistent with the regularity of the club activities – nothing is more dispiriting for children than to be offered an activity that only takes place at irregular intervals or – worse – that does not take place at all. Careful consideration about why such provision is desirable, with clear intention and purpose in play, and a full commitment to regular delivery, should be uppermost when making such decisions.

The British Gymnastics Association provides excellent support materials to help this work, including proficiency awards that can bolster interest and performance standards. These should be seen as having potential for use in both curriculum time provision as well as in the gym club and can act as an extra tool for motivating children to raise their overall achievement and enjoyment in gymnastics. The idea of inter-school gymnastics festivals and (potentially) competition is a further extension of the work that can result from a whole school approach to gymnastics provision.

Ideas for promoting a gymnastics movement vocabulary and teaching through themes

Box 4.4 shows a set of suggested approaches and strategies that can service the basic objective of helping each individual to become a more skilful and competent mover. An engagement with others is obviously conducive to promoting shared ideas, but the evaluative feedback that learners engage in is the catalyst for creative ideas to flourish so it is crucial to build such opportunities into planning. This can happen from the observation of the performance of others but also more intimately when working with a partner, or in small groups beginning with threes, fours and then possibly larger groups, depending on the progress made. The outcome of this particular approach and adopted strategy is to promote the inevitable differentiation and variety that will arise and the creativity we seek. There is a careful balance to find here, which centres on the learner-driven response to tasks set, with the teacher in the role of facilitator, guide and instructor.

Floorwork

Use a variety of warm-up/cool-down activities, sometimes reflective of the main theme of a lesson, sometimes a complete contrast. For example, if the focus of the lesson is work on developing balances on a variety of different body parts then a contrasting, lively warm-up and cool-down, including dynamic jumping and controlled landings, would be appropriate to offset the one-paced nature of balance work.

Continuity and progression in floorwork across the age span of 7–14 years is important in maintaining motivation, enthusiasm and enjoyment among learners. Maintaining these aspects is key to improving individual performance and raising standards, and from a perspective that ensures a recognition that learning is moving forwards and gymnastic activity is not just a repetition of doing the same or the same merely in different ways.

Following are ten ideas to promote creative floorwork:

1 Respond to tasks as individuals, with a partner, in small groups of three or four and as teams.
2 Facilitate structured learning – whole body activity, lower body work-specific, upper body work-specific, combined movement work.
3 Set the same task on floor and on apparatus, where possible.
4 Emphasis on increased flow and continuity in work produced.
5 Set upright and inverted (upside-down) actions momentarily held and for increasingly longer periods to exhibit skill, control and flair in the work.
6 Purposefully encourage working on all body parts, at different levels, on different surfaces (inclined/small/large/soft/hard).
7 Move towards, away from, alongside, front to back, back to front, symmetrically, asymmetrically.
8 Use timeframe ideas – set tasks that have to last for 5, 10, 15, 20 seconds, etc.
9 Set a specific number of actions to perform – for example, how many balances to include in a sequence, part on floor, part on apparatus, etc.
10 Vary the pace of actions – slowed down, quickened, showing variety within a series.

Box 4.4 Learning in and through gymnastic activity

Actions, movements and experience – children and pupils become more knowledgeable and more skilful in being able to show an ever-increasing variety and repertoire of the following:

Travelling – running, hopping, skipping, galloping, walking, stepping, on toes, on a variety and combination of body parts, crawling, sliding, slipping, twisting, turning, springing, bouncing

Balancing – on a range of different body parts, making different shapes, in upright and upside-down positions, on a range of different surfaces, dynamic and static

Jumping and landing – one-foot, two-feet take offs, alternate take-off foot to landing foot; similarly for landings, onto and off surfaces, over surfaces

Rolling – variety of forwards, backwards, sideways, with different shapes – long, tucked, twisted, stretching, curling, twisting, long, wide

Rocking – forwards, backwards, transferring weight

Linking and joining actions to make different sequences – sometimes with a limited number of actions, sometimes more complex, sometimes the same movement done in different ways, sometimes defined, sometimes not

Directions – forwards, backwards, up, down

Pathways followed – straight, circling, diagonal, zigzagging

Speed – slow, medium, fast, but always controlled when moving through space or on/over apparatus, with pauses, showing skill in stopping and maintaining stillness before moving off again

Levels – high, low, medium, face-up, face-down

Swinging, climbing, hanging – using bars, ropes, trapeze, hoops, combinations

Cooperative work – observation, listening to others, evaluating, improving performance

Apparatus work

As a starting premise, we need to accept that children and pupils enjoy and want to work on different apparatus structures that test and pose a set of challenges to their existing skill competencies. It is an integral part of gymnastic learning that as children grow and become stronger they need the challenges that a well-stocked apparatus provision gives them.

When selecting suitable apparatus arrangements – appropriate to the age, ability and prior experience of children being taught – your awareness of what is practicable and achievable within the constraints of available equipment is of prime importance. Knowing the potential benefits to children who are developing knowledge and extending ideas of how to use apparatus as an extension and further challenge to floorwork is crucial to keeping the learning forward-moving and the motivation levels high. The focus here is to maximise the potential benefits of apparatus usage in the pursuit of work that ultimately sees pupils increasingly achieve more refined, repeated, and longer series of actions and movements, making increasingly complex movement sequences both on the floor and using apparatus as cited in PE National Curriculum documentation.

Key considerations here are:

- Is the arrangement safe? Is the class being taught able to use the apparatus safely? Do they have the necessary skill to cope with the set-up? Can they work independently (or with a partner, or as a member of a group when that is the task requirement)? Can they all work simultaneously, even when working on the same apparatus structures?
- Is the apparatus arrangement suitable for the work or theme being covered?
- Will the class be given equal experience of using all the apparatus available over the period of time the particular gymnastics unit of work is being followed?
- Will a range of organisational arrangements be used with teaching groups?

Key points within this for you to remember are:

- Arrangements of apparatus must have sufficient space. Apparatus should not be positioned either too close to walls or doors, or too near to other groups of apparatus arrangements (space permitting).
- Guidance will be needed for younger age groups about suitable starting points for their particular apparatus, that is, where they should attempt getting on to apparatus surfaces. They might be required to follow particular routes and be given certain exit points. They should, in such cases, be given guidance on how to return to their starting points without unduly hindering the ongoing work of other group members. Specific routes around the apparatus might need to be advised.
- Work on avoiding unnecessary queuing. The target is to maximise the amount of movement activity within a lesson, and to this end children should be encouraged to share their particular set of apparatus, and to develop the skills that help them to do just that.
- Children should be taught to become increasingly aware of what others are doing as well as themselves and to use the particular skills that help them to effect this.

- In certain situations it might be necessary to group children according to ability or confidence levels and to give increased exposure to certain pieces of apparatus (height considerations, levels, surfaces, etc.).

Appropriate apparatus should be selected so that the theme that has been explored and developed on the floor can be suitably challenged further by the greater demands that different surfaces, levels of platforms and pathways present. If, for example, the theme is *levels* then the apparatus selected should encourage work to that purpose, therefore arrangements where all pieces are at the same height would not be suitable for this theme. Similarly, where different pathways are being considered, the arrangement must allow for a variety of approaches onto and away from the apparatus and this clearly has implications for the amount of room that will be needed around each apparatus set-up.

The reality of individual context (and being ever mindful of the variation of settings where gymnastic activity takes place, particularly in primary schools), the size of the workspace available, and the amount of apparatus to hand rarely makes it possible to have as many identical arrangements as one would like once more complex and challenging work comes into play. Initial low-level work on apparatus may well involve all groupings on a mat and a bench, but if key objectives are to further challenge, maintain motivation and enthusiasm, as well as increase the quality of the work produced, then the strategies to be used by teachers need to reflect this and simultaneously seek to vary and change composition and arrangements, producing as a result a different response in answer to tasks set.

The following possibilities, and as shown in Boxes 4.5 and 4.6, are put forward for consideration in meeting these demands. They include suggested apparatus arrangements, selected according to what is most suitable for the work being undertaken.

Same apparatus or type of apparatus/same task

This is possible when there is sufficient apparatus available or when group numbers are comparatively small, for example with benches, box-tops, planks and linking equipment.

TASK

Move onto, along, across and off your apparatus using hands and feet only and on different body parts.

Different apparatus/same task

For example, four groups with two different heights of nesting tables and mats, a box and mats, wall-bars and inclined plank/bench and climbing frame.

TASK

Travel over, across, through, along or under your apparatus using a variety of body parts and surfaces.

Two different types of apparatus/two contrasting tasks

For example, three groups on wall-bars/climbing frames with inclined benches, planks and mats; and three groups on combinations of boxes, nesting tables, agility tables and mats.

Box 4.5 Apparatus progression and development

Setting up/Laying out[a]
Initially teacher-directed, increasingly allowing choice and child-driven decision-making
- Using apparatus as individual pieces
- Linking two or more pieces together
- Rotating groups around the set-ups
- Arranging groups in areas for assembly of apparatus
- Allocating specific groups to get out particular pieces of apparatus
- Allocating groups amounts of apparatus to construct own layouts in defined areas
- Using task cards depicting amounts and types of apparatus with activity tasks appended
- Free use of 'whole hall/gym' layouts, where the class decides where individual apparatus pieces go and how they link (for particularly skilled, knowledgeable and experienced classes)

Note
a Groups of variable sizes organised according to age, ability and experience, to set up apparatus in areas allocated.

Box 4.6 Gymnastic themes appropriate to Key Stage 2 and Key Stage 3

At KS2 specifically:	At KS2 and into KS3:
Use of space	Sequences
Transferring weight	Levels
Joining movements	Partner/Group work
Directions	Flight
Parts together and apart	Pathways
Lifting and lowering	Symmetry and asymmetry
Shape	Balance and continuity
Speed	Flow
Twisting and turning	Strength and lightness

A strategy to ensure continuity and progression across the Key Stages – we should be prepared to repeat and therefore consolidate previously covered work, to cover tasks and themes that have been visited already in a variety of different ways and utilising different approaches, including increasingly child-driven decisions within this context. This will entail different task-setting in floorwork, and alternative ways of teaching through a fuller utilisation of organisational methods on the apparatus (to include different layouts and ways of organising the children in their usage of portable and fixed equipment).

TASK

Use the wall-bars/climbing frames to make a sequence, showing transference of weight without flight, and use the boxes to get on/off or over, showing flight either onto or off the apparatus.

Eight groups, four types of apparatus/same task

For example, two groups on boxes and mats, two groups on nesting tables and mats, two groups on climbing frame and mats, two groups on rope sections and mats.

TASK

Use your apparatus to show twisting, turning, stretching and curling movements and actions.

Eight groups, four types of apparatus/different task

Groupings as in example above.

TASK

Show twisting movements and actions on climbing frame and rope sections, and use boxes and tables to show turning movements.

Different apparatus arrangements/different tasks (for experienced classes)

For example, first group on wall-bars, inclined benches and mats; second group on rope section, box, bench and mats; third group on agility table, benches leading towards and away, mats; fourth group on different heights of nesting tables, planks and mats.

TASK

Use the wall-bar arrangement to make up a sequence as a group showing assisted flight and balance; use the rope arrangement to make an individual sequence that shows flight and balance; use the agility table layout to make a group sequence that shows flight; use the nesting tables arrangement to make up a sequence in pairs showing flight with matching actions.

In the above examples there is ample opportunity to vary the work for each individual child in an open-ended form of task setting – note the emphasis on personal interpretation, potential for shared planning and performance, and giving vent to creativity and flair within the work produced. Groups can be rotated around the different set-ups within sessions, time allowing, or in subsequent sessions as the work develops and progresses.

Follow-up activities in the classroom could involve children in mapping exercises of their particular apparatus arrangement of the day, and promoting thinking about alternative structures for the next session. Involvement of this type, beyond the confines of the gymnastics lesson itself, helps to promote the thinking and creative process and at the same time reinforces the principle of learning across cognitive, physical and affective domains.

Assessment criteria – applicable at Key Stages 2 and 3

Observation and assessment

A basic and integral assessment tool to be employed by all teachers teaching all aspects of PE is the ability to observe, analyse and evaluate what children are doing in their lessons. Essentially, this can be summarised under four key headings:

1 *Is the class working safely?* With care, under control, in response to tasks set.
2 *Is the class answering the task?* Listening, understanding, appropriateness of response, challenge.
3 *How well is the task being answered?* Appropriateness of the idea(s), quality of performance.
4 *How can the teacher help?* Feedback/further guidance, clarification, teaching points, demonstration, discussion, suggestion, praise/encouragement/criticism/reflection on the effort.

The above can lead to overall evaluation of performance out of the observation, interpretation and assessment of how the individual child/pupil has met the aims of the lesson or overall learning objectives. This, therefore, leads quite naturally into informing where work needs to go next for the class as a whole, sets up planning the content of the follow-up lesson and can also identify particular tasks for individual children that will progress their learning specifically.

Keeping records

Recording and keeping written records on children's performances on a regular basis helps teachers to keep track of coverage of the work undertaken and also provides detail of individual performance over time. This can ultimately lead to summative commentaries on the individual pupil and also set the markers for future provision, and for where the work in the area needs to progress to next. Class record sheets are a useful mechanism for this (Figure 4.2), but these need to be both manageable and appropriate for the purposes they serve.

We are well aware of the importance of keeping records, not just to help us with future planning, but also as testimony to the provision of quality learning experiences. They also serve the practical purpose of informing end-of-year reporting procedures. On a week-to-week/lesson level, in terms of recording class (and individual children's) performances, the following markers are suggested:

• Have a clear picture of what you want to assess – is it the class as a whole, individuals, particular skills, responses generally to tasks set?
• Identify which children you wish to focus on for recording purposes – make this manageable, say no more than four or five children each session, enabling coverage of the whole class across a (say) 7-week period (which may well tie in with a specific unit of work).
• Keep a general record of what is covered in a session, as well as notes on the particular children chosen for observation.

Assessment and recording of pupil progress		
Pupil name	**By the end of the relevant Key Stage pupils should be able to:**	**Comments**
	Plan • plan extended sequences of at least 5 or 6 movements joined together and including changes of speed, shape and direction and performance at different levels on floor and apparatus	
	Perform • skills – perform selected gymnastic skills which increasingly show clear body shape, extension, accuracy and control • skills – sequence selected actions which are linked together with increasing control, flow and continuity • skills – complete extended, repeatable and more complex sequences which have defined start and finish positions • skills – perform gymnastic actions that match the context, e.g. floor to apparatus, individual, pairs or group work	
	Evaluate • using given criteria, provide accurate and insightful feedback to self and others • identify accurately the component parts and features of a sequence • comment on the quality of actions in relation to speed, direction, and body shape achieved	
	Health • display increasing knowledge of which particular activities are suitable for gymnastics warming-up • understand the need to combine pulse-raising activity and stretching exercises for warm-up and warm-down parts of each lesson	
	Safety • safely apply lifting, carrying, siting, assembly and dismantling of apparatus skills • safely share the workspace and the apparatus with due concern for own and others' safety	
	PSHE • work collaboratively and cooperatively with others • display understanding and sensitivity for others' abilities	
Key 1, Working towards; 2, Achieved; 3, Achievement 'plus'		

Figure 4.2 Key Stage 2/Key Stage 3 gymnastics.

- Make reference in your records where relevant of organisation, who worked with who, which groups worked on which apparatus, and so on.
- If it helps, use a template under three headings – what the children learnt, what I learnt and where the work goes next.

Please note that what is advocated here is a procedure to follow for *all* PE lessons so that the overall picture of children's physical development, competence and skill level is mapped. From this base a fully informed, and therefore accurate, analysis of how children have performed across the year is achieved, which supports feedback to colleagues for future reference, parents and the learners themselves.

Equipment

To ensure that effective delivery of the statutory requirement for gymnastic activity can take place, the following lists represents a checklist of apparatus to meet this objective. This should also assist schools when considering their own particular needs and help to identify specific priorities when looking to purchase or procure further apparatus.

Fixed apparatus (wall-hinged)

Climbing frame(s) to include linking bar(s), beam(s), ladder(s), rope/swinging attachments, etc.

Portable apparatus (including linking equipment)

- Sets of nesting/activity tables;
- movement table;
- benches (wooden/padded);
- wooden agility planks/other linking equipment (e.g. 'storming planks' and 'bird perches');
- mats (enough for at least one between two), size and weight to suit the whole age range (remember that mats come in different shapes and colours, which can lend much to usage and apparatus layouts);
- trestles (A frames, etc.);
- stools;
- boxes – section and bar;
- balance beam(s); and
- springboard(s).

Additionally, it is always useful to use other traditional PE equipment, such as skipping ropes, cones, skittles, bean bags and hoops, to present alternative challenges and tasks using equipment familiar from other activities. They lend colour, and different shapes can combine to make different types of structures around which children can move. They can also serve the very useful and practical purpose of adding to what might be a limited provision of typical or more formal gymnastic equipment.

Bibliography

Coates, B. (2005) *Inspirational Gymnastics for Key Stage 2* (CD-ROM). Hayling Island: Brian Coates.

DfEE (1999) *Physical Education in the National Curriculum*. London: Department for Education and Employment/Qualifications and Curriculum Authority.

DfES (2007) *The Early Years Foundation Stage*. London: Department for Education and Skills.

Hall, J. (1996) *Gymnastic Activities for Juniors*. London: A&C Black.

Malmberg, E. (2003), *Kidnastics: A Child Centred Approach to Teaching Gymnastics*, Leeds: Human Kinetics.

Mitchell, D., Davis, B. and Lopes, R. (2002) *Teaching Fundamental Gymnastics Skills*, Leeds: Human Kinetics.

Pickup, I. and Price, L. (2007) *Teaching Physical Education in the Primary School – A Developmental Approach*. London: Continuum.

Price, L. (2003) *Primary School Gymnastics – Teaching Movement Skills Successfully*. London: David Fulton.

Chapter 5

Creative approaches to promoting healthy, active lifestyles

Jo Harris

Introduction

The promotion of healthy, active lifestyles among children and young people is a long-standing and frequently stated aim of PE programmes in schools. All teachers of PE would like to think that they have helped motivate pupils to adopt an active lifestyle that benefits their health and enhances their quality of life. However, active lifestyles are not as prevalent among children and young people as we would like to think. Indeed, up to a third of children lead sedentary lifestyles and choose to avoid physical activity in their free time. Clearly, there are many reasons for this trend towards sedentary living (such as increased access to transportation and energy-saving gadgets, and concerns about children being safe playing outside). However, we need to face up to the fact that it may also be partly because PE in schools is not sufficiently engaging for a minority (but still a large number) of children. This may be due to narrow curricula dominated, for example, by traditional games activities and/or a limited range of didactic teaching styles in which pupils predominantly follow teachers' instructions. It is important, therefore, that schools reflect on the effectiveness of their current programmes in terms of turning children 'on' to activity and helping them to integrate it into their everyday lives.

In order to help combat the trend towards sedentary living and increases in childhood and adult obesity, the government's review of PE is focusing much attention on pupils learning about the value of healthy, active lifestyles and them being helped to make informed choices about lifelong physical activity. This requires clarification of the knowledge base and creative approaches to the pedagogies which help pupils value and adopt healthy, active lifestyles.

Creative teaching and learning

Creative teaching and learning can be subdivided into three inter-related themes: teaching creatively, teaching for creativity and creative learning, which collectively represent the characteristics of good teaching. Consideration of these themes and their key characteristics is particularly helpful when considering how to effectively promote healthy, active lifestyles as it prompts teachers to think 'outside the box' in terms of helping young people change their activity behaviour. Tables 5.1, 5.2 and 5.3 present each theme in turn, with a selection of their key characteristics and examples associated with the promotion of healthy, active lifestyles among young people.

Table 5.1 Teaching creatively to promote healthy, active lifestyles

Teaching creatively: using imaginative approaches to make learning more interesting, exciting and effective	*Examples associated with promoting healthy, active lifestyles among young people*
Being an inspiration	Enthusiastic teachers of PE who clearly love their subject and are good role models as they demonstrate healthy lifestyles (e.g. eating healthy foods, walking/cycling to work). Teachers who motivate and encourage learners and who are able to make PE fun and satisfying for all pupils, irrespective of their physical ability
Knowing your subject	Teachers of PE who appreciate that promoting healthy, active lifestyles involves more than simply telling children that being active is good for them. Teachers who appreciate that children need to understand why this is so and need to believe it by experiencing enjoyable PE lessons in which they learn the 'why, how, what and where' of physical activity
Making connections	Teachers who appreciate that promoting healthy, active lifestyles is more effective if approached as a whole-school activity. Teachers who help pupils make connections between related learning in PE; science; personal, social and health education; and food technology (e.g. about healthy weight management and energy balance)
Stimulating curiosity	Teachers who encourage children to think about issues such as enhancing well-being and quality of life and the contribution that physical activity can make to this at all stages of life. Teachers who make links to online materials, such as the interactive websites for pupils on the 'healthy schools' website, which help children think about health in a holistic and meaningful way
Being encouraging	Teachers who empower pupils by encouraging a 'can do' attitude to PE and who reward and celebrate their pupils' positive achievements. Teachers who understand that many individuals choose not to be active in their own time as they consider themselves to be 'not the sporty type' or 'no good at PE/sport'
Allowing time	Teachers who make best use of the PE time available to them and include a broad range of activities to help them achieve key aims such as encouraging lifelong activity
Exploring teaching styles	Teachers who are prepared to experiment with different delivery styles to achieve the desired effects. They feel privileged to be in a position to challenge, inspire and motivate pupils and will work hard to find effective ways of doing this

While some teachers may feel constrained by official documentation as they consider it to limit their ability to teach creatively, effective teachers tend to view official documentation, such as the National Curriculum, as merely a framework within which a multitude of possibilities exist.

Table 5.2 Teaching for creativity to promote healthy, active lifestyles

Teaching for creativity: intentionally incorporating activities in lessons which permit learners to be creative	Examples associated with promoting healthy, active lifestyles among young people
Planning	Teachers who plan for learners to explore the differences between 'moderate' and 'vigorous' intensity activity, to think of and design examples of each and link this to the recommendation for young people to be moderately to vigorously active for one hour every day
Questioning	Teachers who use a hierarchy of questions to assess learning at different levels, for example:
	- Describe how you feel when you skip
	- Tell me what is happening to your body
	- How could you increase your heart rate further?
	- Can you explain why this happens?
	- What other activities cause this to happen?
	- Can you create a series of four different activities which make your heart rate go up, then down, then up again, etc.?
Types of knowing	Teachers who use questions to help pupils understand their own thinking. For example: The media is stating that children are becoming fat and unfit. What do you think about this? What makes you think this? What do you think are the reasons for this? What can be done about it?
Group work	Teachers who encourage pupils to work with others to create solutions to tasks/problems. For example: Task – work as a group to design and perform a circuit of four exercises which will strengthen major muscle groups in different parts of your body (arms, legs, abdominals, back).
Learning metaphors	Teachers who actively involve pupils in their own learning. For example: Task – choose three out of six activities (jogging, skipping with a rope, bench stepping, galloping, brisk walking, astride jumps) and spend 2 minutes on each. Afterwards, describe and explain the effects of the different activities on your body (e.g. heart rate, breathing rate, temperature, appearance, energy balance, muscles)

A whole-school approach to the promotion of healthy, active lifestyles

A whole-school approach to the promotion of healthy, active lifestyles should involve the creation of an ethos and environment that support and encourage physical activity for all members of the school community. Every school should be working towards achieving 'Healthy School' status, which requires schools to meet compulsory 'physical activity' criteria, including:

- having a whole-school physical activity policy – developed through wide consultation, implemented, monitored and evaluated for impact;
- consulting with pupils about the physical activity opportunities offered to them at school, identifying barriers to participation and seeking to remove them;

Table 5.3 Creative learning to promote healthy, active lifestyles

Creative learning: learning to think in new ways and connecting learning with knowing	Examples associated with promoting healthy, active lifestyles among young people
Process and product	Teachers who actively involve pupils in the process of learning and emphasise that it is the journey which matters as much as the destination, for example increasing pupils' activity levels is more important than making them fit; an over-emphasis on making them fit could put them off activity
Experiential	Teachers who involve pupils in learning through doing, for example show me (rather than tell me about) an exercise/activity to ... tone up your stomach muscles; help you use up lots of energy; stretch your calf muscles; help you relax
Cross-curricular	Teachers who form links between subject areas, for example involving pupils in an authentic cross-curricular project to research for and design a new play area for a primary school which includes areas to facilitate and encourage physical activity
Imagination	Teachers who are willing to try different ways of working and to 'let go', for example allowing pupils to choose from a range of activities (e.g. aerobics, step, circuits, aqua-fit, tai-chi) and to decide how they would like their progress to be assessed in these activities (e.g. activity diaries, fitness tests, ability to perform with good technique, understanding of key principles, a combination of these methods)
Nurture/Development	Teachers who capture children's imaginations through unusual ideas, for example answering questions using actions only; designing active party games using only balloons and string
Enabling conditions	Teachers who ensure that pupils have the freedom or 'space' to try out their ideas and to undertake 'trial and error' processes; that is, understanding that you can't make an omelette without breaking a few eggs!

- providing opportunities for all pupils to participate in a broad range of extracurricular activities that promote physical activity;
- encouraging pupils, parents/carers and staff to walk or cycle to school under safe conditions, utilising the school travel plan; and
- giving parents/carers the opportunity to be involved in the planning and delivery of physical activity opportunities and helping them to understand the benefits of physical activity to themselves and their children.

These clearly provide a plethora of opportunities for creative approaches to the school environment, the curriculum, the out-of-school-hours learning programme, and travel to and from school.

An important feature of a whole-school approach is the promotion of a clear and consistent message about how active children and young people should be, which is 'one hour a day'. The recommendation in more detail is that:

All children (aged 5–18 years) should take part in physical activity of at least moderate intensity for one hour per day. Those who currently do little activity should take part in physical activity of at least moderate intensity for at least half an hour a day. In addition, at least twice a week, all children should take part in activities that help to develop muscular strength, flexibility and bone health.

While the 'one hour a day' message is straightforward to communicate, the full recommendation may need further explaining to ensure that it is clearly understood. For example, 'one hour a day' refers to accumulating 60 minutes of activity per day, which can be made up of two 30-minute blocks, four 15-minute blocks, six 10-minute blocks or even ten 6-minute blocks.

Physical activity includes PE lessons, sports and dance clubs, exercise and training sessions, active play and recreation, as well as walking, cycling, skateboarding, rollerblading, and physical jobs around the home such as housework and gardening. It is important that children recognise that everyday activities (such as walking and cycling to school) are included in this recommendation. These activities are referred to as 'routine' and 'habitual' and can make a significant contribution to the overall amount of activity an individual does.

Moderate-intensity activity makes participants feel warm and slightly out of breath. A typical example of a moderate-intensity activity is brisk walking. 'Intensity', however, is a personal perception and what feels 'moderate' to one person might feel 'light' (easy) or 'vigorous' (energetic and demanding) to another. Most activities can be performed at different intensities. For example, 'slow walking' or 'strolling' is low- or light-intensity, while 'brisk walking' is moderate-intensity, and 'fast walking', 'power walking' or 'race walking' would be described as vigorous-intensity activity. The recommendation includes both 'moderate-intensity' activity and 'vigorous' activity. Vigorous activity is energetic and feels demanding; it makes participants feel hot and increases their heart and breathing rates.

Activities that develop muscular strength, flexibility and bone health involve controlled lifting and lowering of all or part of one's own body weight and are commonly known as weight-bearing activities. These include activities such as climbing, jumping, skipping, gymnastics, dance, aerobics, circuits, and sports such as basketball and volleyball. Weight-bearing activities such as climbing, skipping and jumping often feature in children's play, while older children are likely to engage in more structured forms of exercise such as performing body conditioning or resistance exercises and stretches in aerobics, step, circuits, multi-gym or personal exercise sessions.

The strengths of the physical activity recommendation for children and young people are that it is:

- simple to understand (and to communicate);
- age appropriate (i.e. different from the adult recommendation);
- flexible (i.e. it involves accumulating time and a whole range of different physical activities);
- differentiated (for the already active and the inactive); and
- comprehensive (it involves a range of components such as aerobic capacity, muscular strength/endurance, flexibility).

The recommendation should be used in the following ways:

- to promote a clear and consistent public health message about physical activity;
- to set realistic and attainable targets – an hour a day for those already active, half an hour a day for the inactive; and
- to support individuals in their efforts to meet and exceed their targets.

The contribution of the physical education curriculum to the promotion of healthy, active lifestyles

The PE curriculum can clearly make a major contribution to the promotion of healthy, active lifestyles, through children and young people:

- experiencing a broad range of physical activities;
- becoming more physically competent;
- increasing their confidence in a physical activity context;
- feeling good about themselves and having fun;
- learning about the value of physical activity to health, fitness and well-being;
- learning about how active they should be and where they can be active in school and in the community; and
- learning about themselves and their ability to make decisions, reflect, improve, be creative, self-manage, work with others and be independent.

The quality of teaching and learning about healthy, active lifestyles tends to be variable in schools, depending on the knowledge and interest of the teachers involved. Some teachers enthusiastically inject health and fitness information into most of their PE lessons while others overlook it and focus almost entirely on developing skills, techniques and tactics. Clearly, a balance is needed to ensure that children become more skilful and confident movers and experience a broad range of physical activities, but also understand the importance of being active, how active they should be, and where they can be active in school and in the community.

Table 5.4 presents an interpretation of the learning associated with the promotion of healthy, active lifestyles. It is aligned with the requirements of the National Curriculum for PE and incorporates links with relevant health-related aspects of subjects such as science, personal, social and health education (PSHE) and food technology. In order to clarify the range of coverage and the progression between Key Stages, the learning outcomes are placed into four categories: safety issues, exercise effects, health benefits and activity promotion.

It is interesting that, of the four categories of 'health and fitness' learning outcomes, the outcomes that are more frequently and effectively delivered within PE are those relating to 'safety issues' and 'exercise effects'. In other words, teachers are generally good at ensuring that children learn about safety in lessons (e.g. tying back long hair; removing jewellery; warming up) and that they learn about the changes that occur when they are active (e.g. feeling warmer). However, the learning outcomes which are less frequently delivered in PE are those relating to 'health benefits' and 'activity promotion'. This suggests that children are not necessarily learning about the range of benefits of activity (e.g. in relation to healthy weight management; psychological well-being; stress relief; bone health and osteoporosis) or about how active they should be, where they can be active, and how to put together a personalised exercise programme. Yet this learning is vital to the promotion of healthy, active lifestyles.

It is, therefore, important that the PE curriculum teaches all children about the 'one hour a day' recommendation and includes some monitoring of activity levels for children to determine whether or not they are meeting the recommendation. This can lead to valuable discussions about how children can get more activity into their everyday lives. The setting up of personalised activity diaries with specific targets should help motivate children to find ways of increasing their activity levels. A personalised activity and fitness education is clearly desirable.

Unfortunately, however, health-related learning in PE is sometimes narrowly interpreted as vigorous activity, warming up or fitness testing. These narrow interpretations have the potential to lead to undesirable practices such as 'forced' fitness regimes, directed activity with minimal learning, inactive PE lessons involving excessive teacher talk and/or dreary drill. Unfortunately, these are more likely to turn young people off, rather than on to, physical activity.

Effective delivery of health-related learning involves more than just passing on information to young people. Knowing the benefits of physical activity is not sufficient to affect behaviour change. Many children and young people know that activity is 'good' for them but they do not do enough activity to gain health benefits. They need to be motivated to be active and to be helped to feel good about participating. The ways in which health-related information and experiences are delivered to young people is critical. Pupils should enjoy their involvement in physical activity. They should be presented with opportunities to make progress, succeed and feel confident about being active. In essence, we want young people to 'love being active'. They should also be encouraged to help others to develop a positive, 'active' image of themselves.

Cross-curricular links and thematic approaches

Children should learn a great deal about health, physical activity and fitness across the curriculum; for example, they should learn the benefits of an active lifestyle, how the body functions, where to be active and how much activity they should do. This learning features in several places in the curriculum, particularly in the subjects of physical education, science, and personal, social and health education. In PE, for example, primary school pupils learn how important it is to be active, how exercise affects the body in the short-term, and why physical activity is good for their health and well-being. Secondary pupils learn how to go about getting involved in activities that are good for their personal and social health and well-being, and how to monitor and develop their own training, exercise and activity programmes in and out of school. This learning should take place within a broad and balanced programme that enables all pupils to experience a range of activities, with each area of activity covered in sufficient depth for pupils to develop competence, confidence, appreciation and understanding.

In science, primary school pupils learn that taking exercise and eating the right types and amounts of food help humans to keep healthy and they learn about the effect of exercise and rest on pulse rate. Secondary pupils learn about the need for a balanced diet, that food is used as a fuel during respiration to maintain the body's activity, and the role of the skeleton and joints in movement. In PSHE, primary school pupils learn

Table 5.4 Learning about healthy, active lifestyles

		Safety issues Pupils can:		Exercise effects Pupils can:
Key Stage 1	a	identify and adhere to safety rules and practices (e.g. changing clothes for PE lessons; tying long hair back; not wearing jewellery; sitting and standing with good posture; wearing footwear when skipping with a rope; no running fast to touch walls)	a	recognise, describe and feel the effects of exercise, including changes to: i breathing (e.g. becomes faster and deeper) ii heart rate (e.g. heart pumps more quickly) iii temperature (e.g. feel hotter) iv appearance (e.g. look hotter) v feelings (e.g. feeling good, more energetic, tired) vi external body parts (e.g. arm/leg muscles are working)
	b	explain that activity starts with a gentle warm-up and finishes with a calming cool-down	b	know that the body uses food and drink to release energy for exercise
Key Stage 2	a	explain the need for safety rules and practices (e.g. adopting good posture at all times; being hygienic; changing clothes and having a wash after energetic activity; wearing footwear for some activities; following rules; protecting against cold weather; avoiding sunburn in hot weather; safe lifting; sensible use of space)	a	explain and feel the short-term effects of exercise: i the rate and depth of breathing increases in order to provide more oxygen to the working muscles ii the heart rate increases to pump more oxygen to the working muscles iii the temperature increases because working muscles produce energy as heat and the skin can become moist, sticky and sweaty because the heat produced by the muscles is transferred to the body's surface (skin) so that body temperature is controlled iv appearance can become flushed as blood vessels become wider and closer to the surface of the skin v feelings and moods can vary (e.g. having fun and being with friends)
	b	identify the purpose of a warm-up and cool-down, and recognise and describe parts of a warm-up and cool-down (i.e. exercises for the joints (e.g. arm circles), whole body activities (e.g. jogging, skipping without a rope) and stretches for the whole body, such as reaching long and tall or parts of the body, such as the lower leg or calf muscles)	b	explain that the body needs a certain amount of energy every day in the form of food and drink to function properly (e.g. for normal growth, development and daily living) and that body fat increases if more food and drink is taken in than is needed (e.g. for breathing, growing, sleeping, eating, moving, exercise)

		Health benefits		Activity promotion	
		Pupils can:		*Pupils can:*	
Key Stage 1	a	explain that regular exercise improves health by:	a	identify when, where and how they can be active at school (in and out of lessons)	
	i	making you feel good (e.g. happy, pleased, content)	b	use opportunities to be active including at playtimes	
	ii	helping body parts (e.g. bones and muscles) to grow, develop and work well			
Key Stage 2	a	explain that exercise strengthens bones and muscles (including the heart) and helps to keep joints flexible	a	monitor their current levels of activity (e.g. during a weekday and a weekend day)	
	b	explain that exercise can help you to feel good about yourself and can be fun and sociable (e.g. involves sharing experiences and cooperating with others)	b	identify when, where and how they can be active in school and outside	
	c	explain that regular exercise permits daily activities to be performed more easily	c	make decisions about which physical activities they enjoy and explain that individuals have different feelings about the types and amounts of exercise that they choose to do	
	d	explain that being active helps to maintain a healthy body weight	d	use opportunities to be active for 30 to 60 minutes every day (with rest periods as necessary), including lessons, playtimes and club activities	

continued on next two pages

		Safety issues Pupils can:		Exercise effects Pupils can:
Key Stage 3	a	demonstrate their understanding of safe exercise practices (e.g. tying long hair back and removing jewellery to avoid injury; adopting good posture when sitting, standing and moving; performing exercises with good technique; having a wash or shower following energetic activity; using equipment and facilities with permission and, where necessary, under supervision; administering basic first aid; wearing adequate protection such as goalkeeping gloves and leg pads for certain activities; coping with specific weather conditions, such as using sunscreen to avoid burning in hot weather and drinking fluids to prevent dehydration; procedures associated with specific activities)	a	explain and monitor a range of short-term effects of exercise on the:
			i	cardiovascular system (e.g. changes in: breathing and heart rate; temperature; appearance; feelings; recovery rate; ability to pace oneself and remain within a target zone)
			ii	musculo-skeletal system (e.g. increases in muscular strength and endurance and flexibility; improved muscle tone and posture; enhanced functional capacity and sport/dance performance)
	b	demonstrate their concern for and understanding of back care by lifting, carrying, placing and using equipment responsibly and with good technique	b	explain that appropriate training can improve fitness and performance and that different types of activity affect specific aspects of fitness (e.g. running affects cardiovascular fitness)
	c	explain why certain exercises and practices are not recommended (e.g. standing toe touches; straight leg sit-ups; bouncing in stretches; flinging movements) and be able to perform safe alternatives (e.g. seated 'sit and reach' stretch; curl-ups with bent legs; holding stretches still; performing movements with control)	c	explain the differences between whole body activities (e.g. walking, jogging, cycling, dancing, swimming) that help to reduce body fat and conditioning exercises (e.g. straight and twisting curl-ups) that improve muscle tone
	d	explain the value of preparing for and recovering from activity and the possible consequences of not doing so, and be able to explain the purpose of, plan and perform each component of a warm-up and cool-down (i.e. mobility exercises, whole body activities, static stretches) for general activity (e.g. games) and for a specific activity (e.g. volleyball, high jump)		
	e	perform with good technique developmentally appropriate cardiovascular activities and strength and flexibility exercises for each of the major muscle groups		

	Health benefits Pupils can:	Activity promotion Pupils can:

Key Stage 3	a explain a range of long-term benefits of exercise on physical health:
	
	   i reduced risk of chronic disease (e.g. heart disease)
	   ii reduced risk of bone disease (e.g. osteoporosis)
	   iii reduced risk of some health conditions (e.g. obesity, back pain)
	   iv improved management of some health conditions (e.g. asthma, diabetes, arthritis)
	
	b explain that exercise can enhance mental health and social and psychological well-being (e.g. enjoying being with friends; increased confidence and self-esteem; decreased anxiety and stress) and that an appropriate balance between work, leisure and exercise promotes good health
	
	c explain that increasing activity levels and eating a balanced diet can help to maintain a healthy body weight (energy balance equation) but the body needs a minimum daily energy intake to function properly, and strict dieting and excessive exercising can damage one's health
	
	d explain how each activity area (athletics, dance, games, gymnastics, OAA, swimming) can contribute to physical health and to social and psychological well-being (e.g. it can improve stamina, assist weight management, strengthen bones, be enjoyable)
		a access information about a range of activity opportunities at school, at home and in the local community and know ways of incorporating exercise into their lifestyles (e.g. walking or cycling to school or to meet friends; helping around the home/garden)
		
		b reflect on their activity strengths and preferences and know how to go about getting involved in activities
		
		c participate in activity of at least moderate intensity for a minimum of half an hour and preferably for one hour every day (i.e. 30 to 60 minutes accumulated over the course of a day)
		
		d participate at least twice a week in activities which help to enhance and maintain muscular strength and flexibility and bone health (e.g. dance, aerobics, skipping, games, body conditioning, resistance exercises)
		
		e monitor and evaluate personal activity levels over a period of time (e.g. by keeping an activity diary for 4 to 6 weeks and reflecting on the experience)

what makes a healthy lifestyle, including the benefits of exercise and healthy eating, and how to make choices that affect their health and well-being. Secondary pupils learn about what influences health, how to make safer choices about healthy lifestyles, and the consequences of the decisions about their personal health. At both primary and secondary level, pupils set personal goals in relation to health behaviours.

It is important and makes good sense that 'health-related learning' within and across subjects is identified and 'mapped' and that all teachers make explicit links within their subjects to 'cross-curricular' themes. Indeed, with some creative thinking, numerous curriculum areas can contribute to the promotion of healthy, active lifestyles. References have already been made to cross-curricular links with PSHE, science and food technology. Examples in other subjects are suggested below:

- mathematics – use of pedometers to measure steps per day/week and analysis of this data to monitor individual and group progress over time;
- geography – mapping, compass work and orienteering in the local area; environmental issues around city/town/village planning for physical activity and safety (e.g. for cycling, walking); leisure, sport and recreation in cities, countryside, seaside resorts; local walks to examine urban and recreation planning.
- history – leisure, sport and recreational trends and patterns over the years; history of sport; women in sport.
- IT – using search engines to explore local physical activity and sporting opportunities; compiling and creating a physical activity directory using multimedia; recording and analysing physical activity and physical fitness data;
- languages – the leisure, recreation and sporting habits of the country; physical activity, fitness and sports vocabulary; discussing own physical activity and sporting interests, likes, dislikes;
- design and technology – designing and making 'active' equipment (e.g. target games, skipping rope, frisbee, kite, miniature sailing boat); designing active clothing;
- art – designing physical activity promotion posters; compiling and creating a physical activity directory; painting 'active' murals around school and playground markings for various games/activities; and
- music – different forms of dance music; 'action' music (i.e. music to move to); music, rhythms and dances from different cultures.

Creative teachers can help pupils to make connections between the subjects and may prompt thematic approaches to the curriculum such as 'Healthy Lifestyles', 'Fitness and Food', 'Healthy Weight Management' and 'Energy Balance – Calories in and Calories Out'.

Conclusion

Educating children about physical activity and promoting lifelong participation cannot be 'left to chance'. Children do not automatically develop the knowledge, understanding, skills, behaviours, attitudes and confidence that lead to regular participation in physical activity. These need to be taught and this teaching must be planned and thoughtfully delivered. In other words, we cannot hope that it will be 'caught', rather we need to ensure that it is 'taught'. Physical education currently needs to re-think its philosophy, content and pedagogy in order to more effectively engage with children and young people, motivate them to adopt healthy, active lifestyles and thereby contribute to their health and well-being. Creative approaches to teaching and learning will help achieve this.

Bibliography

Cale, L. and Harris, J. (eds) (2005) *Exercise and Young People: Issues, Implications and Initiatives.* Basingstoke, Hampshire: Palgrave Macmillan.

Cale, L. and Harris, J. (eds) (2005) *Getting the Buggers Fit.* London: Continuum.

DfEE and QCA (1999) *Physical Education. The National Curriculum for England.* London: Department for Education and Employment/Qualifications and Curriculum Authority (available at www.nc.uk.net).

DoH (2005) *National Healthy School Status: A Guide for Schools.* London: Department of Health Publications.

Elbourn, J. (2002). *Aerobics and Circuits for Secondary School Pack.* Leeds: Coachwise Limited (available at www.1st4sport.com).

Fautley, M. and Savage, J. (2007) *Creativity in Secondary Education.* Exeter: Learning Matters.

Harris, J. (2000). *Health-Related Exercise in the National Curriculum. Key Stages 1 to 4.* Champaign, IL: Human Kinetics.

QCA (2007) *Curriculum Review. Physical Education.* London: Qualifications and Curriculum Authority (available at www.qca.org.uk/curriculum).

Websites

National Healthy Schools Programme	www.healthyschools.gov.uk
Galaxy-H (for 7- to 11-year-olds)	www.galaxy-h.gov.uk
Lifebytes (for 11- to 14-year-olds)	www.lifebytes.gov.uk (for 11- to 14-year-olds)

Chapter 6

Information and communications technology in physical education

An innovative teaching and learning approach

Nigel Clarke

Introduction

Although PE teachers have been using information communication technology (ICT) for years within their teaching, it is only since the National Curriculum (1999) made its integration into Key Stage 3 PE teaching statutory that teachers have heightened their awareness of its possibilities. ICT use in PE is not as radical an idea as it first appears. The use of whistles, stopwatches, tape-measures, photographic equipment, video and audio cassettes has been widespread for several decades or longer. More recent emphasis on health-related fitness within the curriculum has led to the recruitment of skin-fold callipers and heart-rate monitors. In all cases the primary role for the particular piece of equipment is to '*communicate information using technology*', whether that be to stop a game (e.g. to communicate an infringement of the rules to the players), or communicate an assessment of how fast an athlete has performed or how hard they have worked. It is, however, the rapid advances in digital technology that have offered the modern PE teacher the opportunity to champion the role of 'trail-blazer' within the teaching profession. Our subject, having teaching and learning opportunities for auditory, visual and kinaesthetic learners, perhaps lends itself to recent advances in ICT better than many other curriculum areas.

Reasons for employing the use of ICT in PE

It is a statutory requirement for the National Curriculum for PE (NCPE) at Key Stage 3. I would also argue that there is an extremely strong case to be made for its inclusion at Key Stage 2, as often children of that age have started to explore ICT both within the other curriculum areas and in their wider life experiences outside school. Key Stage 2 pupils are often more exposed to, and comfortable with, both the technologies and the teaching and learning styles ICT offers than many Key Stage 3 and 4 pupils. With the current focus on Key Stage 2–3 transition, there may be a valid case for capitalising on these ICT experiences by encouraging the Key Stage 2 pupil to take a lead role in supporting their older peers, boosting their self-confidence and esteem and possibly smoothing intra-Key Stage transition.

- It is now commonly accepted as 'good practice' for the PE teacher to select the effective use of ICT to support and enhance their teaching. Indeed, it is comprehensively embedded within the Professional Standards for Teachers Qualified Teacher Status (TDA 2007):

Q17   Know how to use skills in literacy, numeracy and ICT to support their teaching and wider professional activities.

Q23   Design opportunities for learners to develop their literacy, numeracy and ICT skills.

• It supports and complements the DfES *2020 Vision*. This review recommends the need for greater personalised teaching and learning that is both learner-centred and knowledge-centred.

> Learners are active and curious: they create their own hypotheses, ask their own questions, coach one another, set goals for themselves, monitor their progress and experiment with ideas for taking risks, knowing that mistakes and 'being stuck' are part of learning.
>
> (DfES 2007: 6)

Another key point for personalised learning is making the experience assessment-centred for the pupils.

> Techniques such as open questioning, sharing learning objectives and success criteria, and focused marking have a powerful effect on the extent to which learners are enabled to take an active role in their learning. Sufficient time is always given for learners' reflection. Whether individually or in pairs, they review what they have learnt and how they have learnt it. Their evaluations contribute to their understanding. They know their levels of achievement and make progress towards their goals.
>
> (DfES 2007: 6)

One of the key concerns for the PE teacher must, therefore, be how to assimilate this proposed personalised teaching and learning approach into the effective use of ICT in PE. Later in this chapter a case study of just such a situation will be presented.

The world of employment and training into which the current Key Stage 2 and 3 pupils will emerge within the next decade is likely to expect and demand fluency of understanding and usage of the latest communication technologies. The current expansion of motion analysis software, such as Kandle and Dartfish, for work with an ever-increasing range of elite, professional and amateur sports performers and teams, supports this premise. Indeed, the DfES *2020 Vision* goes as far as to say that 'the pace of technological change will continue to rise exponentially. Using ICT will be natural for most pupils and an increasing majority of teachers' (DfES 2007: 9).

There has been a growing body of research evidence since 2000 that documents advantages for both the teacher and learner when ICT is used innovatively within our subject. However, one word of caution should be highlighted at this point. Physical education is still perceived to be a physically literate and practically based subject and the teacher needs to consider this point carefully when integrating ICT into their lesson planning. Just because ICT is available does not mean that it should be used in every lesson! It should only ever be used to support and enhance teaching and learning. It is sometimes easy to become preoccupied with the technology at the expense of the pupils' learning and/or activity levels.

National Curriculum (DfEE and QCA 1999) states that ICT must become an integrated tool of a PE teacher's delivery, yet in Ofsted's report on secondary PE (2000), the lack of ICT inclusion in lessons is regarded as a weakness. With the rapid development in, and availability of, new technologies, coupled with trainee teachers and newly qualified teachers' apparent confidence and willingness to use these (Koh and Khairuddin 2004), the task now becomes the development of this tool in promoting effective teaching and learning. Thomas and Stratton suggest that 'models of good practice are certainly now required to ensure that the best use of ICT is given to pupils' (2005: 26). Bush highlights 'the potential pivotal role that trainees and Newly Qualified Teachers (NQTs) might have to play in disseminating good practice in ICT among their more "experienced" peers' (2004: 49). The current challenge is, therefore, to 'tap into' this enthusiastic knowledge base and provide developmental ideas for the creative use of ICT in PE.

Examples of current ICT use to support teaching and learning in PE

1 The Internet is a knowledge and information resource. Increasingly, teachers' use of it has moved away from traditional search engines towards more focused and appropriately tailored and controlled virtual learning platforms, such as Blackboard and Moodle. These allow the teacher to upload supporting documentation, homework and direct Internet web-links (including video clips), to enhance the pupils' learning experience, onto a readily accessible electronic format. However, care must be taken when using the Internet in a class setting, as often pupils will wander off-task or enter too broad a search term to gain access to the information they need. It can sometimes be beneficial to provide complete address pathways to save unnecessary search time. Another issue when using the Internet as a resource is the current viability of addresses or pathways. These can often lapse or change and necessitate regular checking by the teacher. It is possible to use the pupils to perform this task as part of an introductory task (Table 6.1). The class or PE staff could be provided with a starting list of useful PE Internet sites and asked to carry out the evaluative task suggested.

Table 6.1 The potential of the Internet in physical education

Explore and critically evaluate the key features of your selected websites for group presentation. You may wish to consider features such as: ease of navigation, 'user-friendliness', graphic design and visual impact, usefulness and accuracy of content, how it might be used by a PE teacher (e.g. as a teacher resource or interactively with pupils) and what Key Stage it is most appropriate for.

Web address	Brief description of site	Reference information for pupils	Interactive resources for pupils	Resources for teachers, e.g. video clips	Lesson plans, schemes of work	Evaluation of site

2 Software can support the teacher in administration, communication, lesson planning and resources, record-keeping and assessment. Many teachers will already be routinely using Microsoft programs such as Access, Excel and Outlook Express to ease their administration and communication burdens. Word and PowerPoint particularly lend themselves to information presentation in a format not normally encountered by the pupils in PE lessons. Pupils can use their own cross-curricular ICT skills to produce PowerPoint resources for sharing among their peers, an easy way of producing a 'class library' of electronic knowledge resources. This becomes widely available if burned onto CD or uploaded onto the school's or department's intranet or virtual learning platform. An example of a screen-shot from such a PowerPoint presentation on introducing football formations to Key Stage 2 and 3 classes is given in Figure 6.1; a screen-shot addressing the 'acquire and develop' key strand using a reciprocal teaching approach for cricket is given in Figure 6.2; and the menu screen from a GCSE anatomy and physiology resource PowerPoint presentation is shown in Figure 6.3.

3 Key Stage 3 and 4 pupils, particularly those studying GCSE PE, often enjoy interactive presentations in the format of topical gameshows such as *Who Wants to be a Millionaire?* This can be a particularly useful revision format for the end of a block of work. Again, the pupils could be set a particular topic to revise and produce their own presentations to share as a whole-class resource. The first slide from such a GCSE revision interactive PowerPoint presentation is shown in Figure 6.4. PowerPoint templates for formats such as *Who Wants to be a Millionaire?* are readily available on the web for pupils to use.

4 – 3 – 3

➤The 4 – 3 – 3 formation is usually adopted by teams who have good attacking qualities.

➤For example, Chelsea use this formation as they have very skilful attacking players.

➤This formation is very similar to the 4 – 5 – 1 formation as both wingers maybe asked to help out with defending too.

Figure 6.1 Screen-shot of PowerPoint slide introducing football formations.

The Set-up: Batting Grip

Back to Main

Key Points

- Hands together, middle of the handle.
- V's formed by thumb & forefinger of both hands to be in alignment, running between the outside edge and splice of the bat.
- The top hand should have a slightly firmer hold on the handle than the bottom for control.

Method of Teaching

1. Lay the bat on the ground (face down) with the handle pointing towards batsman.
2. Ask the batsman to pick the bat up, by placing his left hand (Right hand batsman), then his right onto the handle (Will be opposite for left handed batsman).
3. Check V's of thumb and forefinger for alignment & feel for slightly different gripping pressures from top to bottom hand.
4. See Video opposite ⟶

Double click Picture to view Video

Figure 6.2 Screen-shot of a PowerPoint slide introducing how to hold the bat, aimed at Key Stage 3 pupils.

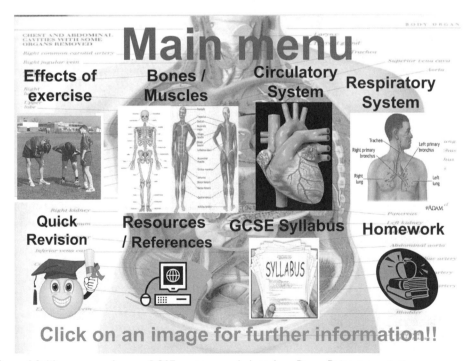

Figure 6.3 Menu screen from a GCSE anatomy and physiology PowerPoint presentation.

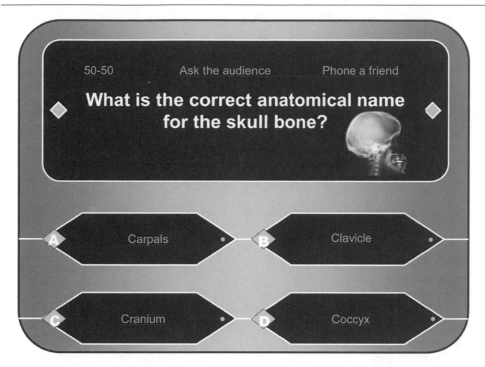

Figure 6.4 Screen-shot from an anatomy and physiology version of the popular quiz show.

4 With the improved user-friendliness and accessibility of software video-handling and editing packages such as Windows Media Player and Movie Maker, PE teachers are now offered a novel opportunity to download and construct their own video libraries as an additional teaching and learning resource. This offers a plethora of innovative opportunities for younger teachers in particular, who may well be experienced in the digital video age possibilities of social electronic networks such as YouTube and Facebook. It is now possible to start or intersperse a lesson with video clips of elite or peer performances of the skills, techniques or tactics being investigated within that lesson. Movie Maker can also provide a particularly strong motivational and inspirational message with its ability to link moving video images with text and overlay the whole production with a suitably motivational music track. The London 2012 Olympic bid contained just such inspirational images and was widely attributed with being a key attribute in the successful final presentation to the candidate city selection committee. Possibilities exist for PE teachers to produce their own short presentations using Movie Maker as a promotional tool for a variety of audiences, for example, for Year 9 options evenings when promoting PE as a GCSE/BTech option, as an assembly theme to celebrate an extracurricular success or introduce a visiting speaker, or to publicise the work of your PE department at a Year 6 open evening.

5 The increasing rate of advances in computing power and quality of digital video capture devices, coupled with decreasing hardware and software pricing, is making the possibility of motion analysis of sporting movements and performances much

more realistic for many schools. The range of digital video camcorders and movement analysis software packages varies in complexity, user-friendliness and cost, from Digital Blue, a very basic recording system but very easy to use and suited to Key Stage 2 use in particular, to the more powerful and expensive Kandle and Dartfish packages, more applicable to Key Stages 3 and 4 (GCSE) and 5 (A level) work. Motion analysis work allows pupils to address the requiremens of the key strands 'acquire and develop', 'select and apply appropriate skills and tactics' and, particularly, 'evaluate and improve both their own and the performance of others'.

One major objective for the use of this technology is to help pupils develop their knowledge and understanding of *what* they are doing and *why* they are doing it.

If you look at the attainment targets across the Key Stages for PE, this is made very evident by the terminology used:

- analyse;
- comment;
- understand;
- improve;
- compare;
- safety;
- tactics; and
- composition.

If used appropriately, ICT can help the children achieve some of the attainment target descriptors. Key questions the PE teacher needs to explore before employing this technology in lessons include:

- Can you and/or the pupils easily use the equipment?
- Is it suitable for all situations/activities?
- Can you link it to other ICT – hardware and software?

6 There is often a perceived negative association with ICT and activity levels of children, linking the current 'Playstation generation' of children with increasing obesity and inactivity levels. However, examples of innovative approaches in many British primary schools encouraging children to do more exercise in combination with computers are becoming more commonplace. Interactive whiteboards and even 'Tamagotchi'-style digital pets are being used in schools to get kids moving and encourage activity. Picklenash Primary School in Gloucester decided that they wanted to test the boundaries of what they could use interactive whiteboards for. 'Wake and Shake' workshops, using whiteboards to display a DVD of simple, repetitive aerobic exercises, were developed to be integrated into the pupils' daily routine. The children and teachers do the exercises in their classrooms every afternoon and this helps the school to hit their targets for physical activity.

7 In another electronic innovation, Fizzees, a new 'Tamagotchi'-style digital pet, is being developed to help tackle childhood obesity and motivate children to get fit and healthy. The wrist-worn Fizzee, a prototype technology devised by education

innovator Futurelab, is a character that is nurtured and developed through the activity undertaken by the child wearing it. The device measures heart rate and motion, and uses a scoring system based on recommended exercise levels for young people to determine the health of the Fizzee. The less exercise undertaken by the wearer, the less healthy the 'pet' becomes; however, the more exercise undertaken, the healthier the digital 'pet'.

8   Current success in re-engaging previously disaffected American high school pupils into participating in PE lessons has 'tapped into' their enthusiasm for interactive aerobic-style dance sessions that link a dance mat to a computer screen. This provides further evidence of the powerful potential of ICT for PE.

An opportunity to change the way we teach?

The advent of these new technologies, both within the school environment and in the wider outside world, does present PE teachers with the opportunity to reflect on the way the subject is taught. There is a real chance to explore a new pedagogical approach to the range and types of teaching and learning strategies employed. The digital, electronic era could offer pupils a move away from the traditional 'skills-based', command style of teaching and learning towards a more independent, self-discovery approach wherein the pupils become more involved in the ownership of their own learning. This empowerment of pupils, with greater responsibility for their own learning, is supported by *Every Child Matters* (2005), currently a significant educational issue. It may, however, require an uncomfortable change in role for some PE teachers towards that of a facilitator if personalised, independent learning is truly to take place. There are, however, advantages to be gained for both the teacher and pupils. With much greater interaction by the teacher with individuals/small groups, many of the whole-class management issues may be avoided. It would also necessitate an adjustment from the pupils as they adapt to a 'learning to learn' teaching approach. More of these ideas will be presented in the following case study of just such an approach.

A novel teaching and learning approach for physical education – a case study

This case study describes a novel teaching and learning approach for addressing the knowledge, skills and understanding in the Programmes of Study (PoS) within the National Curriculum for PE (NCPE). In particular, it focuses on the four key strands of:

*   acquiring and developing skills;
*   selecting and applying skills, tactics and compositional ideas;
*   evaluating and improving performance; and
*   knowledge and understanding of fitness and health, while incorporating an innovative and interactive use of ICT within PE lessons.

The use of interactive digital video discs (iDVDs) by pupils as an independent teaching and learning strategy has been developed by Kirkbie Kendal School in Cumbria and used since 2005 as an alternative teaching strategy. The school wanted to move away from the traditional teacher-led skills approach to teaching and learning and encourage the pupils to take more responsibility for their own learning. It was hoped that this would encourage better communication skills within the groups as they would be involved in greater peer coaching and assessment and lead to a better understanding and knowledge of the 'evaluate and improve' key strand. It was also felt that the medium of iDVDs would help both the pupils and staff feel more comfortable with the assessment process in terms of National Curriculum attainment levels (Figure 6.5).

I first became aware of this creative use of DVD technology as a parent when my son enthusiastically told me about his analysis and evaluation role within his lesson and accurately described what attainment level his performance represented and what he needed to do to reach the next level! He was comfortably using technical language and terminology that I and many of my PE colleagues could only ever dream about our trainees using. This new skill he had developed quickly manifested itself in swimming and tennis club sessions, prompting me to instigate a deeper study of what was happening. The school is now evaluating the impact of this method in a collaborative case study with University of Cumbria as part of a jointly funded Teaching Development Agency (TDA) and Association for Physical Education (afPE) innovation grant.

Kirkbie Kendal School, located in South Lakeland, is a rural, co-educational comprehensive of approximately 1,100 pupils, aged 11 to 18 years, and is in partnership with the University of Cumbria through its initial teacher training programmes. Kirkbie Kendal's PE department contains an advanced skills teacher (AST) for ICT in PE who has pioneered a pedagogical shift away from the traditional 'skills approach' to PE

Figure 6.5 Using badminton DVD.

teaching towards a more independent and reflective strategy using the interactive medium of mobile DVD players. The typical class size of thirty has approximately ten mobile DVD players available per lesson that operate from the integrated battery that provides sufficient charge for several lessons. The DVD players are simply recharged from the mains electricity supply via a series of adaptors ready for next use. Like most electronic devices, the quality of these mobile DVD players is rapidly improving and the price is becoming more accessible for schools. Current good quality DVD players with 7-inch screens similar to those used at Kirkbie Kendal are available for under £100 each. The iDVDs provide guidance through examples of correct technical models for skill development (using video clips of either elite performers recorded from television, or high-level school performers recorded using a digital camcorder), selection of appropriate skills and/or tactics for the appropriate situation and explanation of NCPE attainment levels in 'pupil speak' for assessment purposes. Figure 6.6 shows the DVD player being linked to a plasma screen to introduce a whole class to attainment levels. Currently, DVDs for four curriculum activities are used: athletics, cricket, badminton and health-related exercise, although I am aiming to develop other areas. These are targeted at the Key Stage 3 and 4 audiences and are also suitable for GCSE practical work. The iDVDs are produced using a digital video editing software package that is commercially available to buy for approximately £250 (Adobe Encore DVD2) and Adobe Photoshop is used for editing most of the artwork/photos used in the DVDs.

An additional aim of the case study was to provide some continuing professional development (CPD) that aims to provide the University of Cumbria PE trainees and

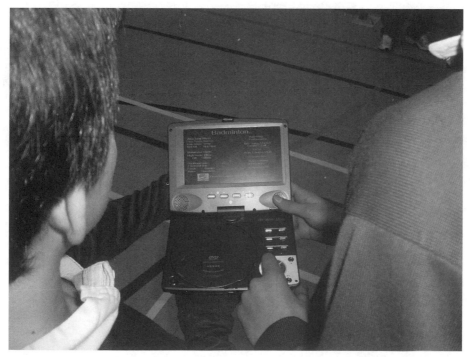

Figure 6.6 Plasma and DVD setup.

partnership schools' PE staff with an understanding of and effectiveness in delivering *personalised, independent learning opportunities* for their pupils and subsequent use of alternative assessment models, through the media of iDVDs. There are others who have investigated electronic methods of supporting practical activity areas, for example, Ying and Koh (2006) have presented an online approach to the teaching and learning of gymnastics. The iDVD approach does, however, allow for more individualised and portable learning opportunities to occur.

This case study has the additional bonus of allowing PE trainee teachers to significantly experience several of the professional standards for the award of Qualified Teacher Status (QTS); for example, the need to be creative, as mentioned specifically in the Personal Professional Development standard: 'Have a creative and constructively critical approach towards innovation, being prepared to adapt their practice where benefits and improvements are identified' (Q8).

This project will also address trainees' competencies in areas mentioned specifically within the Professional Knowledge and Understanding standard: 'Know how to use skills in literacy, numeracy and ICT to support their teaching and wider professional activities' (Q17); and the Professional Skills standard: 'Design opportunities for the learner to develop their literacy, numeracy and ICT skills' (Q23) and 'Use a range of teaching strategies and resources, including e-learning' (Q25a).

More significantly, perhaps, it provides an opportunity to combine and assess a successful use of ICT based on familiarity with good practice, firmly aligned to an understanding of how pupils learn, as suggested by Pachler (1999). Learning theories are complex and some may have different applications of ICT to others. The case study illustrates an example of the more constructivist approach of utilising ICT in a discovery-based, problem-solving format. It should also test the findings of Blomqvist *et al.* (2001), who found that a video-based teaching strategy improved both the serving skill and badminton knowledge and understanding of PE trainees, compared to 'traditional' teaching. Underpinning the whole pedagogical process for this independent self-discovery approach is a reliance on the pupils' understanding and following a 'learning to learn' teaching and learning strategy. This is based on the 'plan, perform and evaluate' learning model outlined in Figure 6.7. This model places learning at the middle of the 'improving performance' pathway.

A major part of the case study involved a dissemination of this innovative teaching and learning method to trainee teachers who would then introduce and trial this approach to serving PE staff and their pupils during their final teaching practice.

The project's phases involved:

1 Familiarisation and training for ten final-year secondary PE trainees from the University of Cumbria in both the use of the portable DVD players and the discovery-based, problem-solving teaching style. One school-based workshop session was delivered using Kirkbie Kendal School Key Stage 3 pupils by PE staff from both the school and university, during the autumn term of 2006. A follow-up university-based training session in the use and familiarisation of both the technology and range of iDVD content, including how to integrate its use into lesson planning, was held in March 2007 just before final teaching practice commenced.

2 Use of the portable DVDs and DVD resource by the final-year trainees in their final teaching practice school (March–June 2007), as appropriate. A selection of

Improving performance

Plan: 1. watch elite performer on video or demo of the skill
          2. use visualisation of you performing the skill
          3. perform the skill
          4. decide on corrections to be made
          5. focus on one point at a time
          6. visualise the correct technique again

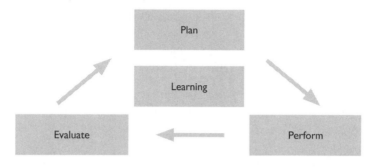

Perform:

Performer: focus on key point – DO IT!
             did it feel better?

Coach: watch key point for correction
             did it improve?

Evaluate: essential for your performer to improve

    1. watch your performer then compare to video clip
    2. spot what they are doing correctly and tell them (praise will encourage them)
    3. give them a level, tell them why they are at that level ... then help them reach the next level
    4. tell them what they need to do to improve
    5. give simple instructions
    6. FEEDBACK must be IMMEDIATE

Figure 6.7 'Plan, perform and evaluate' learning model.

suitable schools and trainees was made by negotiation in advance, taking into account the school's ICT facilities, willingness to participate in the project and strength of the trainee. (This teaching style and resource was only used as one of a range of pedagogical strategies employed by the trainee during the placement.)

3 A review and evaluation of all the participants' experiences of the project including:
    • the trainees' teaching practice reflections;
    • the pupils' perspective on this teaching and learning strategy compared to other methods of delivery; and
    • the partnership PE staffs' impressions on their pupils' response and on the effect on their learning.

4 Production of the case study DVD resource and supporting CPD in its use, for distribution to the University of Cumbria partnership schools.

The aim was to introduce, in a very hands-on way, an innovative teaching and learning approach to the university's final-year secondary PE trainees, using the media of iDVDs. Ten trainees spent a day working with school staff and pupils observing the personalised and individualised strategy being delivered to Year 7 and 8 pupils. During the lunchtime break the trainees gained some experience of using the technology themselves and critically evaluated, with school and university staff, this method of 'teaching' compared with other, more traditional, methods (Figures 6.8 and 6.9).

Two of the many positive comments offered by the trainees on the lessons they observed were:

> I was amazed how on-task the pupils remained, with absolutely no class management issues arising.

> All the pupils I worked with had a really well-developed ability to meet the 'evaluate and improve' key strand.

The study has just been completed at time of going to print and is currently in its review and evaluation phase following completion of the PE trainees' final teaching practices. The study has examined the impact and experiences these trainees and their pupils had with this creative and novel use of the iDVD technology and the teaching approaches pioneered at Kirkbie Kendal School. Among the early initial findings is a strong level of enjoyment expressed by the pupils experiencing this teaching and learning approach for the first time. Other key features identified include large improvements perceived by pupils in their knowledge and understanding of the

Figure 6.8 Trainee use with pupils.

Figure 6.9 DVD use.

'acquire and develop' and 'evaluate and improve' key strands, the NCPE attainment levels and how to progress to next level.

Some of the comments provided by the pupils include:

> We got to coach other people, which helped with our knowledge; we had good examples as well instead of just teachers.
>
> (Female, Year 10)

> You could keep replaying the skill and work at your own speed. It also showed it in slow motion, a breakdown of the skill making it easier to learn.
>
> (Female, Year 10)

> Liked being left to find things out for myself.
>
> (Female, Year 10)

> We could see what we needed to achieve to get so many marks . . . to get 21–25 marks you have to . . .
>
> (Female, Year 10, GCSE)

> Miss let us work on things we need to improve instead of people all doing the same.
>
> (Male, Year 10, badminton club)

> We had more freedom to teach ourselves and experience how to improve and guide someone else.
>
> (Female, Year 9)

It is, however, worth pointing out that both the experiences of the trainees and their pupils reinforce the following recommendations for this teaching approach at this early stage:

- Not for every lesson.
- Not for every class or pupil.
- Useful as another teaching and learning approach to add to the teacher's repertoire.
- Benefits in encouraging greater responsibility for own learning.
- Encourages and develops cooperative peer teaching and learning.

Recommendations

What does the future hold for ICT in PE? In answering this question it is safe to surmise that ICT in PE is not going to disappear. In fact, given the new QTS Professional Standards for Teachers (September 2007), the recent QCA (2007) review of the curriculum for Key Stage 3 and the DfES (2007) *2020 Vision* report, the influence and impact of ICT use in PE teaching is likely to grow considerably. This will inevitably have a consequence for the PE teaching profession, which will be forced to evaluate current teaching and learning strategies in light of these new technological demands and expectations. Pressure will increase to develop creative and innovative uses for the new technologies as they come 'online'. Physical education teachers should not fear this expectation but rather see it as an opportunity to develop and experiment with new skills and challenges. Many of the technologies, including the hardware and software packages, are becoming more user-friendly, with better tutorial support available on accompanying discs or online. There exists a genuine opportunity that perhaps did not exist in the past for us as a profession to revolutionise the way we teach and move towards truly independent, personalised learning with greater empowerment of pupils for their own learning.

Five top tips

1 Only ever use ICT in PE lessons if it enhances learning. Ours is still a mainly practical subject!
2 It may not be suitable for every pupil, class or activity. Consider the advantages and disadvantages for each lesson.
3 Shop around for the best deals on both hardware and software. Good deals (including free trial periods) are widely available on the Internet.
4 Media projectors are commonly used to project images from computers/laptops onto, for example, sports hall walls. Consider flat-screen plasma TVs as an alternative. They take up little room and can be boxed in for protection/security. It is easy to connect external devices, for example DVD players (see Figure 6.6).
5 Have a go! Try things out and don't be afraid to make mistakes. We learn more from what we get wrong than what we get right. Just make sure you regularly save your work.

References

Blomqvist, M., Luhtanen, P. and Laakson, L. (2001) 'Comparison of Two Types of Instruction in Badminton', *European Journal of Physical Education*, 6(2): 139–155.

Bush, A. (2004) 'Computers and Physical Education Teachers: A Rationale for Use and a Small Scale Study into Physical Education Teachers' Attitudes towards and Use of Computers', *British Journal of Physical Education*, 35(1): 45–49.

DfEE and QCA (1999) *Physical Education. The National Curriculum for England.* London: Department for Education and Employment/Qualifications and Curriculum Authority.

DfES (2005) *Every Child Matters* (available online at www.everychildmatters.gov.uk).

DfES (2007) *2020 Vision.* London: Department for Education and Skills (available online at www.teachernet.gov.uk/publications).

Koh, M. and Khairuddin, A. (2004) 'Integrating Video and Computer Technology in Teaching', *British Journal of Physical Education*, 35(3): 43–46.

Ofsted (2000) *Secondary Subject Report: Physical Education.* London: Office for Standards in Education (available online at www.ofsted.gov.uk).

Pachler, N. (1999) 'Theories of Learning and ICT', in Leask, M. and Paschler, N. (eds), *Learning to Teach Using ICT in the Secondary School.* London: Routledge.

QCA (2007) *Curriculum Review. Physical Education.* London: Qualifications and Curriculum Authority (available online at www.qca.org.uk/curriculum).

Thomas, A. and Stratton, G. (2005) 'What Are We Really Doing with ICT in PE?', *British Journal of Teaching Physical Education*, 36(2): 22–26.

TDA (2007) *Professional Standards for Teachers.* London: Training and Development Agency (available online at www.tda.gov.uk/teachers/professionalstandards/standards.aspx).

Ying, L. W. and Koh, M. (2006) 'E-learning: New Opportunities for Teaching and Learning in Gymnastics', *British Journal of Teaching Physical Education*, 37(1): 22–25.

Chapter 7

Creativity and outdoor education

How dare you

Richard Lemmey

Over the decades the curriculum pendulum has swung periodically between the three 'R's at one extreme and child-centred education at the other. Currently, it may be said to be swinging somewhere in the middle. The proponents of each end of the spectrum have always had some sort of application for outdoor approaches within their particular take on the curriculum; those from the structured content-based extreme have seen the opportunities for character building, teamwork, problem-solving skills and other instrumental skills of relevance to the economy while those at the child-centred end perhaps have appreciated a setting where diverse learning styles can be better catered for by more diverse learning opportunities and where pupils' responses to the environment are explored. There are, of course, to some degree arguments for both perspectives. So as the pendulum has swung, outdoor education has had to adapt its content and delivery to suit the educational mores of the time.

There is a range of provision in outdoor education that mirrors the current prescription of the curriculum as seen in the wider sense. Its more obvious expression is through outdoor centres and the voluntary sector, such as Outward Bound, the Scouts and the British Schools Expedition Society, and locally through clubs both in and out of school. These settings tend to emphasise outdoor skills experience and rely on specialist equipment and remote environments and as a result can sometimes be expensive and exclusive. They have also evolved from a tradition that may now be seen as having issues with gender, target-based achievement and a quasi-military past. The recent history of a very few of these providers has also led to the formation of the Adventure Activities Licensing Authority, which monitors the provision of safe activities for children at outdoor centres.

School-based provision has been growing extensively throughout the UK and the emphasis here tends to be on inclusion of low-risk activities at low costs. Sometimes these activities use the local environment but others can also be carried out within school grounds very effectively. Because of the more dominant perception of outdoor education being 'risk in the wilds', schools, outdoor aspirations may sometimes be hampered by notions that it is dangerous, expensive and with nebulous outcomes.

In order to explore the issue of creativity and the outdoors it is worth listing what may be seen as the component principles of outdoor education. First, and obviously, it must be in or related to the outdoors in some way, whether that be actually being outside or learning about the outdoors in a classroom. Second, the outcomes of outdoor activities are nearly always real and uncertain. In its more extreme manifestations it may even be said to have the possibility of a negative outcome. This uncertainty principle is an important one as, while it introduces reality and the possibility of success or disappointment, which may be seen as desirable, it does make it difficult to reconcile the learning outcomes of a session with the demands of a prescribed curriculum. Good outdoor education may also be said to require use of a wider range of intelligences and physical, mental and emotional skills in one activity than is usually demanded of children. Where the activities take place in particular impressive surroundings there is also the opportunity for a spiritual component as a result of experiencing the natural world, be it seeing a woodpecker or a sunset.

Many of the benefits ascribed to outdoor education may, however, be as a result of other factors than those claimed by its advocates. It may well be that the novelty of many experiences and the new people met is actually what is effective in producing positive change rather than the activities and the knowledge learned. Given this proviso, there are many benefits from learning outdoors, and in any case teaching creatively to maintain the novelty and freshness of experience may be no bad thing.

The opportunities provided by the returning pendulum have been defined succinctly in a document published by the DfES (2006) and interested parties in the outdoor industry as a manifesto for learning outside the classroom, which to some degree can be seen as defining the expectations of outdoor learning. It states:

> When these activities are well planned, safely managed and personalised to meet the needs of every child they can:
>
> * Improve academic achievement
> * Provide a bridge to higher order learning
> * Develop skills and independence in a widening range of environments
> * Make learning more engaging and relevant to young people
> * Develop active citizens and stewards of the environment
> * Nurture creativity
> * Provide opportunities for informal learning through play
> * Reduce behaviour problems and improve attendance
> * Stimulate, inspire and improve motivation
> * Develop the ability to deal with uncertainty
> * Provide challenge and the opportunity to take acceptable levels of risk
> * Improve young people's attitudes to learning.

Not much to ask! The list, though, may be a prompt or checklist when assessing our own provision from a distance. To what degree does our programme achieve these expectations?

For the purposes of this chapter, the intention of this book will be followed by considering how creativity in outdoor and adventurous activity can be used with young people at Key Stage 2 or 3 in a school environment. There are three ways in which creativity may be considered in the context of this setting and it is essential to differentiate among the three. First, there is the creative provision of outdoor activities, then there is the use of outdoor activity to increase the creativity of young people and finally, there is the use of the outdoors to enhance the provision of the creative areas of the curriculum such as graphic art, sculpture or music. To merely provide examples of novel and creative approaches in these areas would be straightforward and teachers could use these with their groups and they would perhaps join the canon of spiders' webs and tree-huggings that have become the caricature of outdoor education. Although examples from these areas will be considered, the intention of this chapter is to show ways in which teachers can develop their own creativity as a meta-skill that will help not only with the three areas but also with other aspects of their work.

Preparation for planning

Providing diverse learning opportunities in outdoor education is key to the inclusion of all children and before planning a session it can be useful to consider briefly what this means. One of the concepts at the heart of this is that of Kolb's learning cycle (Kolb and Fry 1975). This cycle takes people through an experience, a period of reflection, the making of a conclusion that will lead to further planning. Kolb describes the types of learner as activists, reflectors, theorists and pragmatists and each stage suits one of these styles so that each learning style has an opportunity for application. This cycle is sometimes shortened to 'Plan, Do, Review, Apply'. These stages and learning styles should be at the back of our minds in planning, but to attempt to cater for all types of learning style in a session might be optimistic, although in a programme this might be desirable.

In the process of planning any outdoor session there are certain standard components and the essence of this approach to being creative is to identify those components within any given activity, subject them to a number of theoretical transformations and then assess each one as to its practicality. For example, if we take group size as a component in planning orienteering, which is traditionally an individual sport, we could explore what might happen if we set up the experience for groups rather than individuals. One way might be to give one member of the group a map with point features on, such as telegraph poles and trees; another linear features, such as roads and fences; and the third spatial features, such as fields and woods. To navigate effectively all three maps have to be used together. Thus, by changing group size, a creative idea has arisen around accurate communication and cooperation in navigation.

The generic components that may be used in the planning of a session for any given set of outcomes might be seen as:

- group size;
- group type;
- content;
- sequence (timing);
- leadership;
- equipment;
- communications;
- environment; and
- safety.

The transformations that might be attempted may be seen as:

- reduce;
- increase;

- remove;
- replace;
- reverse; and
- substitute.

This can then be made into a theoretical matrix, as seen in Table 7.1.

I stress that this is a theoretical matrix and that you should not necessarily go through the painstaking process of filling it in. However, if I work through an example the process will become clear. Let us stay with the orienteering in the school grounds example, and rather than working with group size let us consider equipment.

How might equipment be reduced?

The only equipment involved is individual maps, master maps, compasses and markers. The questions generated, therefore, are: What happens when we reduce the individual maps? At first sight what does this mean? We could reduce size, detail or number of maps, so what would be the implications of this? Reducing the size of a map does not appear to have a creative possibility but reducing detail might. What if we leave off the buildings from a map and leave just grass and trees or perhaps leave out a section of the map? The nature of the course immediately becomes different. The markers could be reduced, which would primarily mean in size, and so the nature of the course changes further.

How might equipment be increased?

The maps could be increased in detail or perhaps the master maps might be increased in number. How? Perhaps the first part of the master map is at the start and the second master has to be found as part of the course. Is there anything to be gained from increasing the number of compasses? Perhaps not for each competitor, but compass bearings of the next control given as an arrow at each control could confirm bearings or simplify the course, and for a mixed ability group this may be a good idea.

Table 7.1 Theoretical matrix

	Reduce	Increase	Remove	Replace	Reverse	Substitute
Group size						
Group type						
Content						
Sequence						
Leadership						
Equipment						
Communications						
Environment						
Safety						

How might equipment be removed?

Seemingly rather a strange question . . . but would it be possible to have a verbal master map or no markers at points or part of the map missing? Notice that these suggestions sound impractical but also notice how, with a little modification, ideas improve. Describing a course in a landscape to a team might work if the course was simple and the team were given their running maps shortly after the course had been described and they were allowed to ask three clarifying questions. Having no markers and having to give a description of an obvious feature at a location would test confidence, as runners would not be getting confirmation that they were in the right place. Taking a section out of a map will lead to sole reliance on a bearing rather than ground features, and if this is a planned outcome it could be very effective. So, gradually, we further modify our initial ideas into better and better ones.

How might equipment be replaced?

How can you replace maps, markers and compasses? A map might be replaced by a number of photographs showing markers at their locations; a marker might be replaced by a coloured light or a wind chime; and compasses could be replaced by arrows or animal tracks on the ground. Whether you think these ideas are any good is irrelevant. The object is to demonstrate how asking the right questions can help.

How might equipment be reversed?

What if maps were reversed and became reflections of the true map? What if the locations were indicated by the absence of something and what if the compasses were reversed? These are extreme suggestions and are becoming more impractical but can you detect the 'these would work if' thoughts in your head? Work on the idea that a course location could be indicated by the absence of something for a while and see what you come up with.

How might equipment be substituted?

What might be substitutes for maps, compasses and markers? Instead of runners having maps they could have a walkie-talkie to contact a map-reader elsewhere, or maps might be replaced by drawings. A map could be devised by substituting something else for north – perhaps east or the top of a far-off hill. Compasses could be substituted by tracks, and markers could be substituted by manhole covers.

This example has been worked through asking the questions of one component, in this case, the equipment for orienteering. It may be worth trying to assess the creative outcomes if we apply one transformation to all the components. Table 7.2 shows the transformation of 'substitution' as applied to the same situation. Here, an orienteering course has been transformed into a detective trail around a route defined by photographic clues, which have taken the place of a master map, and which is completed when the groups formulate a logical sequence of events that explain the photographs. This can then be embellished into a scene of crime investigation, which, although requiring a lot of preparation, will always then be there on the shelf. The fact that this 'crime investigation' only became apparent as an idea when I was halfway through the process of filling in the table is significant. This demonstrates how organisation is

Table 7.2 Substitution of components

Component	Current practice	Substituted by	Creative practice
Group size	1		3
Group type	Competitive runners		Competitive observers
Content	Marked route		Cryptic route
Sequence	Quickest sequence		Logical sequence
Leadership	Individual		Defined leader
Equipment	Maps, compass, marker		Pictures, lens, digital camera
Communications	Written marks		Groups communicate with a base
Environment	School grounds		Park or inside school
Safety	Running hazards		Supervision

crucial in the creative process and the significance of this is explored later. If we then consider how different learning styles may be applied we can see how more balanced opportunities are provided for Kolb's activists, reflectors, theorists and pragmatists through the cryptic and the logical solution components of the task.

Problem-solving

The manifesto's other example of school-based outdoor work is that of problem-solving. This has a less concrete/active learning-style bias and provides a great opportunity for applying the theory of Kolb's learning cycle since it is easy for groups to go round the cycle of Plan/Do/Review and conclude a number of times if planned accordingly. The transformations can be applied to problem-solving, demonstrating a range of creative opportunities.

To illustrate this, I will subject the popular problem-solving activity involving plank and barrel bridge-building to the process of transformation and explore a number of creative options.

In the activity in Table 7.3 we now have a situation in which two directors make decisions about the task without seeing it and two managers have to describe to the

Table 7.3 Substitution of practice

Component	Current practice	Substituted by	Creative practice
Group size	8		2 + 2 + 4
Group type	Mixed of the same year		Directors, managers, workers. With the directors out of sight of the task but with control
Content	Use equipment to get from A to B		'Buy' from a budget to get from A to B
Sequence	Plan Do Review (Retry)		Direct Manage Build
Leadership	Allow it to evolve		Appointed leaders take turns
Equipment	Planks, barrels		Limited by price
Communications	Free for all		Strictly through managers
Environment	Playground		Indoors and outdoors
Safety	Teacher supervision		Manager responsible for H&S

workers what the decision is as well as feeding back to the directors how things are going. The decisions about the task also involve using a budget to 'buy' priced equipment to achieve the task. This has obvious relevance to workplace awareness and citizenship but adds a pressure and perhaps frustration to a situation where students get very involved and learn much. This can work well either as a cooperative activity or a competitive activity between groups.

Putting the problem-solving into a structure and context such as this makes it much easier to discuss the educational issues that arise. For example, rather than asking a young person 'how well did you communicate' or 'what were the problems of communication', which are frequently asked questions, it is easier to include the emotional dimension by asking 'how did you feel, being a manager and communicating with the workers?' By providing a context, understanding the principle becomes easier.

I would like to draw attention to the component of 'leadership' and, therefore, control in this type of activity. One of the frequent criticisms of such problem-solving activities is that they are contrived and therefore the responses and involvement of individuals require a 'buy in' to the task that sometimes doesn't happen. This may lead to misbehaviour and safety issues. One of the advantages of outdoor education is that it *is* often very real. If you don't hang on to the rope you (or your friend) might fall or if you don't catch properly your friend might get hurt. Generating genuinely real creative activities is difficult because reality in the context of physical activities may well have potentially negative outcomes. This is not to say that they must be avoided – but there should be a progressive build-up before they are attempted. This progressive build-up of reality and responsibility can be developed through giving young people opportunities to make decisions about real activities. So as the Plan/Do/Review/Apply model is used within the outdoor activities, young people have greater influence at each stage.

This gradient of transfer of control has been described in the work of Tannenbaum and Schmidt, who describe a gradient from autocratic leadership through democratic leadership to abdicratic leadership, where control is transferred to the participants. If, as the Manifesto suggests, outdoor activities have an obligation to develop independence, manage uncertainty and accept risks, how else can it be achieved, other than through a progressive handing over of the reins? In the early stages this may be achieved by allowing choice of activity, which later might turn into some input to curriculum design for the coming term. With activities away from the school site such responsibilities become easier to give, involving the group in choice of outdoor venue, activity and how to get there. Getting groups to organise their own transport and menus is very real and with careful supervision need not be a serious safety issue. Where responsibility has started to develop, activities such as 'trust falls' provide good opportunities that can be used within school, given the appropriate mats and numbers of catchers. The teaching of first aid as part of this progression provides a perfect opportunity for young people to develop independence and manage uncertainty.

With larger programmes or periods away from school there is often a tendency to hand over the responsibility for planning and delivery entirely to a skilled Adventure Activities Licensing Authority (AALA) provider. These outdoor centres do a valuable job in giving young people experiences they otherwise would not have but there is sometimes a uniformity about their provision which does not match the diversity of their clients. For some groups, getting away into a completely different setting is a desirable end but for other groups there are opportunities being missed. As a separate bolt-on experience, the likelihood of transfer of lessons learnt back to the school is low and the opportunity for reinforcement of school-based curriculum work is missed.

Working creatively with centres on coordinated programmes is highly desirable in that it results in a better match between the group and the activity. It also stimulates both sets of professionals to extend their experience and expertise. When working on these extended experiences, whether they are home-based activity weeks or centre-based courses, the issue then arises as to how we can be creative in our planning and structuring of the experience.

Metaphorical planning

One way in which we might be creative at this early stage is through the principle of metaphorical planning. This involves the key staff, who know the group and their needs, in identifying a metaphor for the type of experience they intend. By doing so they will, albeit unwittingly, create a situation where the structure of the experience is implicit, as well as the content. For example, take a group where it is felt that each individual has something to give but the group has not developed an identity in itself. Metaphors that might be used in this situation might be a *pilgrimage* or *ship-building*. These two metaphors are quite disparate in their feel but there are situations where both might apply.

The pilgrimage metaphor involves the idea of people meeting to prepare together for a linear journey, which has some sort of deeper symbolism. Upon this journey, if the *Canterbury Tales* are to be believed, there are places where the group stop and an individual takes responsibility for some aspect of the journey. There is no reason why Chaucer's approach of storytelling might be used, but more realistically a more diverse range of skills and tasks could be arranged to give an individual a principal contribution at each site. Between each stop everyone works together but each step has a significance for an individual. The final destination involves all the group in some sort of important symbolic act.

Ship-building, on the other hand, is a process where there is a detailed plan at the start. A notable person lays a keel and groups of people work on different tasks at the same time towards the same single aim. There is a clear two-stage process of building the hull on land, which is then launched by a notable person, and fitting it out before commissioning.

Both these metaphors are obviously not literal models, but they do lead to defined structures. Pondering the pilgrimage metaphor, one is compelled into the questions of 'Could someone storytell?', 'Are there any musicians?' and 'What might be an alternative to storytelling for our group?' In the ship-building analogy, would one have come up with the idea of involving notable people from outside as important visitors to the project? The point is, the specific metaphor may ultimately be rejected but the reasons for the rejection will have come about because of the creative thinking it stimulated in itself.

The use of these metaphors often stimulates the inclusion of other curriculum areas in outdoor education and, in the two examples, the opportunities for art, music, history, geography, maths, English, science, IT and languages can be realised through diary-writing, storytelling, collecting artefacts, recording observations, drawing up plans, speaking to notable people, map-making, and so on.

Examples of metaphors and their characteristics might be:

- Exploration: going to an unknown area without maps. A number of recce groups going on minor trips and bringing back information for a master map. No set final objective.
- Carnival: preparing acts for a major one-off activity for an audience at the end of the period. Needs a circus master.
- Tournament: a series of competitive activities between individuals or teams that take place in front of the 'king'.
- Journey: a linear trip involving preparation for a clear end. Equipment is carried. Sometimes local people are asked for help.
- The Amazon: starting as small individual rivers, the waters come together lower down in a major flow and then slow down and disperse at the estuary.
- Climbing Everest: a prepared journey with a single ultimate objective that passes from camp to camp with tasks of increasing difficulty as the journey progresses.
- Voyage: a single group on a journey in which crew perform different tasks under a skipper. There may be hazards such as pirates, starvation, weather or rocks, so a 24-hour watch is required.

It is not intended that such metaphors are followed slavishly but I hope it can be seen how, for example, the voyage metaphor has produced the idea of a 24-hour watch and how such an activity could provide some wonderful learning opportunities. What the watch is watching for need not be pirates but could be a signal from the next supply of incoming food and goodies at 4.30 am. (As an aside, there is an element of re-inventing the wheel here as the watch was favoured strongly by one Robert Baden-Powell.)

Such metaphorical planning can be used at the one-session scale or over a year's programme. One example of this was at the Lakes School in Windermere, Cumbria, at Key Stage 3, where the transition from primary to secondary school was an issue for a catchment area of both large schools and remote village schools. The project started as a result of observing the differences in approach to problem-solving of students in different settings. In break times, while pupils played fantasy games on computers, staff perceived differences in their approach to virtually the same problem that was part of an English comprehension exercise. Teachers also felt that their responses were usually uncharacteristic of the individuals as they knew them.

From these observations came the question as to how the students would behave if the fantasy situations were in fact real. Initially, some trial experiences involving navigation and problem-solving were run in some nearby woods and the responses of both students and staff were so positive that the possibility of using the outdoor experiences as a theme for the whole curriculum was considered. What transpired was a whole year's curriculum centred on the mythical figure of Matka. Matka lived in the woods and was very shy of adults but was the keeper of the wisdom that young people need to make the most of life; wisdom that led to qualities such as vitality, determination, empathy and compassion. The year then became a process of acquiring the skills that would equip one to meet Matka, who would only make himself visible to those who were ready.

Making fires in the wood, preparing menu sheets, building shelters from builder's plastic, working in groups, writing music, drawing storyboards, identifying animals and finally stalking Matka's messenger's lantern and a cloak through the misty woods at dusk were all part of the year's experience of an integrated curriculum. When these students left the school and were asked what was their most significant experience of school, the single most significant experience was Matka.

I hope these examples demonstrate that creative approaches to outdoor education are possible and can start on quite a modest scale. As confidence grows, the extent of the creativity can widen. These approaches do need time and thought to be perfected, but over time the boxes of props will build up with the lesson notes and be a source of confidence for the future as well as satisfaction with the past. Centres are wonderful at what they do and I have referred to how their use might be optimised, but there is no need to spend a lot of money. Scrounged tarpaulins and bits of rope are cheap and will service many more children than fancy tents. Making a pot-hole in the gym from mats and gym equipment covered in drapes can achieve a great deal without safety problems, expense and long trips in buses. It is not the same as real pot-holing, which does have its place, but it works as a way of creating an exciting and lively PE session.

This chapter does stay with the definition of outdoor education as implicit in the National Curriculum in a PE context, but I would encourage you to find other enthusiasts in other curriculum areas where cross-curricular synergy waits to be released.

Finally, from experience, I suspect that many will turn to this book for in-depth consideration of important theoretical issues, while others – and here I am being autobiographical – might grab it at the last minute looking for inspiration for a session. For both types of reader I would commend one last consideration of the stages in the creative process. These are:

- organisation;
- fermentation;
- inspiration; and
- verification.

I include these because creative inspiration will not come from laboured study of books alone, nor from desperate dipping. The transformation of components I started with illustrates the first stage – the 'organisation'. After this there *must* be a period of fermentation, a time when you allow your subconscious to work. Go for a run, drink beer, eat cake; do whatever takes your mind off it. Then when inspiration comes, write it down (because it doesn't last), then go back to the setting in which you were working – paper at a desk or with colleagues – and try it out, verify it.

I commend all this to you in the certainty that the opportunity for enormous job satisfaction exists and that many have experienced it before you as a result of these approaches. Be inspired and be inspiring!

References

DfES (2006) *Learning Outside the Classroom Manifesto*, Nottingham: Department for Education and Skills.

Kolb, D. A. and Fry, R. (1975) 'Toward an Applied Theory of Experiential Learning', in Cooper, C. (ed.), *Theories of Group Process*. London: John Wiley.

Tannenbaum, R. and Schmidt, W. H. (1958) 'How to Choose a Leadership Pattern,' *Harvard Business Review*, 2: 95–101.

Chapter 8

Cross-curricular Key Stage 2 physical education

Moving to learn

Glenn Swindlehurst

Introduction

The *Primary National Strategy* (DfES 2007) and *Excellence and Enjoyment* (DfES 2003) recognise the importance of a flexible curriculum and that by looking at the whole curriculum schools can make learning a relevant and exciting experience for all children.

Making links between curriculum subjects and areas of learning deepens children's understanding by providing opportunities to reinforce and enhance learning. It does this in a number of ways. One of these is building concepts through providing children with opportunities to meet the same or related information in different ways, adding to the richness of their experience (*Primary Framework for Literacy and Mathematics*, DfES 2006).

Cross-curricular PE could be better described as learning *through* PE or *moving to learn*. It 'uses physical activity as a context for and means of learning. It involves a whole range of learning outcomes, which go beyond learning how to engage in selected physical activities' (BAALPE *et al.* 2005).

Thus, by using physical activity children can learn other skills such as social skills, teamwork, problem-solving, making moral and aesthetic judgements, understanding tactics and strategies of games, and appreciating the relationship between exercise, health and well-being. All these can be delivered through a high-quality PE programme without detracting from the skills children need to develop to participate in physical activity and sport.

This chapter will give examples of how PE activities can support the learning outcomes of other subject areas within the curriculum. These examples could be delivered in the time allocation for that subject, in the time allocation for PE, or in a combination of the two. In essence, it is not about learning how to engage in selected physical activities, but how these physical activities can help children learn and meet the outcomes of other curriculum areas.

How PE activities can be used for theme-based learning and planning within the curriculum will also be explored. The approach is about putting PE at the heart of the curriculum.

The activities that will be explored are:

- dance, narrative writing and theme-based planning;
- games and non-fiction writing;

- gymnastics and ICT;
- outdoor adventurous activities and science; and
- athletics, mathematics and ICT.

Dance activities, narrative writing and theme-based planning

If children can see or experience something for themselves they are more likely to understand it. If their imagination and natural curiosity is stimulated through dance and movement it can be used to develop their learning in literacy. This example will look at how literacy and writing learning outcomes can be delivered through dance activities using the creative dance process.

The purpose of narrative is to tell a story. Narrative is essential for young children and their learning. They develop their understanding through stories and use narrative to organise their ideas, and to structure their thinking and ultimately their writing.

Dance drama tells a story and is performed in narrative style. The story can come from anywhere but must have movement ideas that can motivate both teachers and pupils. Children can also adapt their own stories into dance.

In the primary framework for literacy and mathematics, drama is one of the twelve strands of learning in the literacy curriculum.

Drama

- Use dramatic techniques, including work in role to explore ideas and texts.
- Create, share and evaluate ideas and understanding through drama.

Dance is placed within the PE National Curriculum and aims to help children think about how to use movement to explore and communicate ideas and issues, and their own feelings and thoughts.

There is a crossover between the two arts in terms of how they can be used to support children's understanding of literacy and narrative. Both arts explore ideas through movement although in a slightly different way. They can both communicate how a character feels; drama might verbally communicate, and dance can use body movement to show how the character feels.

One of the problems that can occur with dance drama is that it can turn from dancing into acting to music. The main focus is on developing dance that communicates a story or how characters within a story might move. This might start off like drama as children are initially exploring movement, but it is vital that you move away from literal movement into more dance-like movement, otherwise there is a danger that all dance sessions become an extension of drama. As we have seen above, there is a crossover between the two, but also a clear distinction, and this needs to be made clear in your delivery to children so they understand the difference between the two.

However, using dance drama within literacy time is an excellent way of teaching aspects of literacy and it is important that any emphasis on the performance of the dance drama does not distract from the intended literacy learning outcomes planned.

Theme-based planning

The dance drama is developed within PE lessons and the main learning objectives are explored.

The idea of using a dance drama with narrative was to use the dance structure as a scaffold or framework for writing for children. This is especially important for reluctant writers but can help all children.

Using this dance framework as a focus for narrative writing over a unit of literacy means that the work in the literacy sessions can focus on helping children develop their understanding and improve their writing of settings, characterisation and description before they write the story of the dance drama at the end of the unit.

The literacy sessions will develop the children's writing, whereas the dance sessions help the children experience the story kinaesthetically. This link helps provide an opportunity to reinforce and enhance learning through meeting the story in different ways. At the end of the unit, the children will write out the story of the dance.

> This is a powerful way to represent stories and also acts as a precursor to writing. If children have just acted out or improvised an event they will find writing easier because the key sequence of events can be more firmly fixed in the mind.
>
> (*National Literacy Strategy*, DfES 2001)

Using the dance framework as a scaffold and concentrating on developing characters, settings and description within the literacy sessions and developing the story through dance will help children improve their writing of the dance drama. This could eventually culminate in a class assembly or performance.

To illustrate the idea here I have used the theme of Zombie Nation to teach dance and narrative writing, although there are many opportunities for using narrative writing in other areas of the curriculum, such as history and geography.

In Zombie Nation, the children explore and create monster characters through simple choreographic principles to create a dance phrase and to perform a dance that communicates character and narrative.

The initial stimulus for this dance came from a song called 'Zombie Nation' by Kercraft 400. The idea developed into a nation inhabited by zombies and was the starting point for the dance drama.

The story of the Zombie Nation dance

> After watching a horror film in his bedroom, Ellis took a lot longer to fall asleep that night. The moonlight seemed to be playing tricks in his bedroom as shadows danced across the room. Ellis felt a cold draught on his neck as he wearily opened his eyes. It was pitch black. Where was he? He wasn't in his bed. Ellis felt the damp grass on his toes and started to wonder if he was dreaming, but the smell surrounding him was nothing like anything he had smelt before – it was similar to a mixture of smelly feet and vomit. Suddenly, a deep menacing growl, which

started low then gradually got louder, came out of the dark. Ellis ran away from the noise as fast as he could, not knowing where he was running to but desperately trying to get away from whatever was making that hideous growl. All of a sudden he stumbled onto his face. As he started to scramble back to his feet, two piercing bright orange eyes came into his view and started to draw closer. Ellis tried to scream but nothing came out of his mouth; he screamed as loud as he could but still no noise came out. Ellis shut his eyes and expected the worst.

The story continues along the following lines:

[Character has a nightmare and wakes up in a strange dark place. He hears frightening sounds and tries to run away, trips and falls.]

- Ellis is turned into a monster.
- Ellis is taught the latest monster dance step.
- Ellis goes to the Monster Ball.
- As the sun starts to rise, the monsters seem to gradually disappear.
- Ellis feels himself disappear.
- Ellis wakes up back in his bed.

This story of the dance can then be developed through literacy by concentrating on description of settings and characters' feelings and reinforced through the dance sessions. One example that has been used in the PE and School Sport investigation is to use the dance framework and after each dance session have an extended writing session. The children wrote the part of the story they had just performed through movement. This is another way of enacting the tale.

Dance framework example of Zombie Nation (Tables 8.1–8.4)

- Children decide their characters (one child to four or five monsters).
- Child performs the nightmare sequence.
- Monster characters rise from the swamp and start to meet together.
- Monsters find child and turn them into that monster.
- Child joins monsters and groups create a party sequence.
- Sunrise, monsters sink to floor slowly.
- Child wakes up confused, wanders slowly around and sinks to the floor.

Example of linking dance to literacy with the theme of Zombie Nation

By linking this dance drama to literacy work we can add to children's learning through using the theme within all areas of literacy and also the foundation subjects. This example is for half a term and uses some of the QCA units as a starting point but the dance drama is the stimulus for the theme (Table 8.5 and Figure 8.1).

Table 8.1 Progression 1

Learning objective	Introduction to activity
To explore how a character reacts when placed in a frightening situation	Discuss nightmare and being scared, about been in the dark and any feelings children may have about this. Explain the framework for today's dance, which is waking up in a dark, strange place with strange noises. How would you feel?
To know what is needed for a warm-up in dance	What types of movements would show this?

Tasks	Teaching points	Success criteria
Ask children to run around the space for a count of four as if being chased, on toes, freeze. Use your body as though it is listening for something (not putting hand up to ear)	Watch for other people. Only run for a few steps before changing direction	Children can use body to show a sense of straining to listen for strange noises
Children running and looking behind, changing direction continuously	Do not run when looking behind, look then change direction	Children can make quick sharp turns showing change of direction
Ask children to imagine meeting an obstacle, children stop, turn, continue	Imagine stumbling on a group of monsters. How would you get away without being heard?	Children use good facial expressions
Demonstrate or ask children for suggestions of a range of activities after obstacle, i.e. falling, scurrying away	Create a pathway through this strange land	Children can make quick sharp movements, change of direction, different levels, and facial expression when scurrying within their sequence
Ask children to devise a dance phrase	What is good about X's sequence?	
Devise pathway for: 4 counts run, 4 counts freeze (expression), 4 counts run, meet obstacle, scurry away, 4 counts run, 4 counts freeze then 8 counts sinking into the swamp		
Evaluate examples of good work showing signs of the success criteria		

Table 8.2 Progression 2

Learning objective	Introduction to activity	Success criteria
To explore and create a monster character through simple choreographic principles to create a dance phrase	Explain to children that they are going to look at a number of different monsters that they will find in their nightmare. They are going to create a movement phrase based on how these monsters move. Discuss how a zombie moves. Discuss how a troll might move. What words describe these movements? Use stories, poems, video, etc.	Children show stiff, slow movements
To know why you need to cool down after dance		

Tasks	Teaching points	Success criteria
Ask children to try out different movements that a zombie might make	How does a zombie move?	Children show stiff, slow movements
Ask children to work in pairs to create zombie movements. Try out different examples to the music	Teacher to demonstrate a movement	Children can move in time with music
Ask children to try out different movements that a troll might make	Mirror your movements – one person leads, the other follows	Children can show very slow, lumbering, clumsy, heavy-type movements
Ask children to work in pairs to create troll movements. Try out different examples to the music	Teacher to demonstrate a movement	Children move in time with the music
In groups of four or six create a dance of either trolls dancing or zombies dancing at a party	Mirror your movements – one person leads, the other follows	Children show characteristics of moving as either zombie or troll
Ask children to evaluate each group's dance	In groups devise a dance phrase of meeting up and having a party. How do monsters party?	

Table 8.3 Progression 3

Learning objective	Introduction to activity
To explore and create a monster character through simple choreographic principles to create a dance phrase	Explain to children that they are going to look at how two different monsters are going to move and party. How does a vampire move? How does a serpent move? What words can we use to describe its movements?
To describe and evaluate their own and others dances taking account of the monster character	

Tasks	Teaching points	Success criteria
Ask the children to try out different movements that a vampire might make	How does a vampire move?	Children show quick flowing movements, creepy
Ask the children to work in pairs to create vampire movements. Try out different examples to the music	Teacher to demonstrate a movement	Children can move in time with the music
Ask the children to try out different movements that a serpent might make	Mirror your movements – one person leads, the other follows	Children show slithering snake-like movements
Ask the children to work in pairs to create serpent movements. Try out different examples to the music	Teacher to demonstrate a movement	Children can move in time with the music
In a groups of four or six create a dance of either vampires dancing or serpents dancing at a party	Mirror your movements – one person leads, the other follows	Children can show characteristics of moving like a serpent or vampire
Ask the children to evaluate each group's dance	In groups devise a dance phrase of meeting up and having a party. How do monsters party?	

Table 8.4 Progression 4

Learning objective	Introduction to activity
To perform a dance that communicates character and narrative	Discuss putting together all the work they have done so far into a narrative
To describe and evaluate their own and others' dances, taking account of the monster character	In groups they will have to decide who is going to be the child and who is going to be what monster character

Tasks	Teaching points	Success criteria
Children decide their characters		Group decide on characters
Start of dance: child performs their sequence from session 1. As music starts, monster characters rise from the swamp and start to meet together		
Monsters find child on floor and turn the child into one of them		
Child joins monsters and groups create a party sequence		
Monsters sink to floor slowly as music comes towards the end		Party sequence showing characteristics of monsters' movement
Child wakes up confused, wanders slowly around and sinks to floor as music comes to a stop		Completed dance
Evaluate groups' work, refine and practise		

Table 8.5 Example of half term timetable: Zombie Nation

	Week 1	Week 2	Week 3	Week 4	Week 5	Week 6
Dance	Progression 1	Progression 2	Progression 2/3	Progression 3	Progression 4	Progression 4
Literacy	Non-fiction instructions	Non-fiction instructions	Fiction – Narrative Phase 1	Fiction – Narrative Phase 2	Fiction – Narrative Phase 2/3	Fiction – Narrative Phase 3
ICT	Short focused task 1	Short focused task 2	Short focused task 3	Short focused task 4	Integrated task	Integrated task
Science	Moving and growing	Moving and growing	Moving and growing	Moving and growing	Moving and growing	Moving and growing
PSHE	Managing my feelings	Managing my feelings	Managing my feelings	Managing my feelings	Managing my feelings	Managing my feelings
Art				Story of a dream	Story of a dream	Story of a dream
DT	Moving monsters	Moving monsters	Moving monsters			

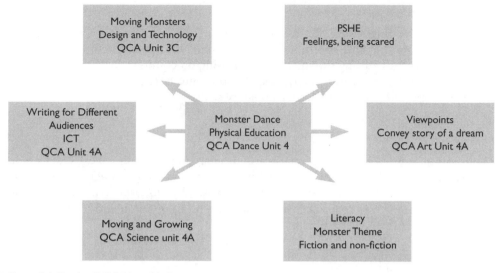

Figure 8.1 Dance QCA Unit 4 links

Literacy work

The non-fiction instruction unit from the Primary Strategy 2006 has three phases, with oral or written outcomes and assessment opportunities at regular intervals.

- Phase 1: Reading and analysis of instructional texts.
- Phase 2: Oral rehearsal; analysis; note-making and drafting.
- Phase 3: Writing and evaluating instructional texts.

The work for this part of the unit revolves around recipes and instructions for craft activities (links with the 'Moving monsters' unit). The children will devise their own recipes for 'Vampire Curry' or 'Serpent's Surprise' and write a set of instructions on how to make the recipe.

Stories set in imaginary worlds is the second of four narrative units in Year 4 Primary Framework for Literacy. The unit has three phases, which have oral and written outcomes including a quest or adventure narrative in the fantasy or science fiction genre. The unit can be linked to other curriculum subjects, and in this example is the Zombie Nation dance drama.

Phase 1

Read, compare and contrast a range of texts with fantasy settings. Identify common features and themes from the narratives. Discuss how settings influence the reactions of characters. Express opinions about the mood and atmospheres created by different authors of narratives with fantasy settings.

Phase 2

Create fantasy settings using photo-editing software. Use images to discuss character responses to settings. This will link with the art unit 'Viewpoints, story of a dream'. Construct a narrative using the images and drawing on common features and themes of stories set in fantasy settings. Organise the story into paragraphs and identify how cohesion is created within and across paragraphs.

Phase 3

Demonstrate how to organise the narrative into paragraphs using cohesive devices to connect ideas. Children write their own narratives arranged into paragraphs, ensuring that ideas are linked within and across paragraphs. The children write their version of the dance drama using the framework and concentrating on the mood, atmosphere and emotions of the main character.

1998 Framework objectives covered:

> Year 4, Term 2: T1 – how writers create imaginary worlds; T2 – how settings influence events, incidents, characters' behaviour; T3 – compare settings; T4 – use of expressive, descriptive language; T8 – review range of stories; T10 – develop use of settings in own writing; T12 – collaborate to write stories in chapters; T13 – write own examples of expressive, descriptive language.

ICT – writing for different audiences

Short focused task 1

Technique: to alter font size and use effects to indicate relative importance.

- Ask class to list food that a troll, serpent, vampire or zombie might like.
- Demonstrate how to change font size, bold, underline, italics, word art, and so on.
- Divide the class into small groups and ask each group to resize the words to indicate their order of priority for favourite foods for a monster.

Short focused task 2

Technique: to use cut and paste to reorder a piece of text.

- Prepare a file of a mixed-up recipe for Vampire Curry or Serpent's Surprise.
- Demonstrate how to use cut and paste to reorder the recipe.
- Ask children to reorder the recipe into the correct format.

Short focused task 3

Technique: to delete, insert and replace text to improve clarity and create mood.

- Enter a short descriptive passage from literacy, provide children with a copy of the text. Discuss how some of the words create moods.
- Demonstrate how to delete, insert and type over words.
- Ask children to modify the passage to change the mood.

Short focused task 4

Technique: to use a spell checker and to amend text using find and replace.

Integrated task

Objectives: to use ICT to organise, reorganise and analyse ideas and information and to edit text and use a variety of presentation techniques. This task could be the front page of a newspaper of a monster attacking the school, a wanted poster for a monster or an advertisement for a vampire slayer.

Science: QCA Unit 4A – Moving and growing

Through this unit children learn about the skeleton and how it is related to movement and support in humans. It looks at what happens to the skeleton and muscles as they move. It also compares human bones and skeletons with those of other animals. Comparisons could also be made with monsters; for example, zombies cannot bend their knees and elbow joints very well so how does that affect how they move? What sort of a skeleton does a troll have? How can a vampire look like a human but change into a bat?

Personal, social and health education: Managing my feelings

The first dance session investigates waking up in a nightmare and feeling scared, which could be investigated further in PSHE. Additionally, materials from the social and emotional aspects of learning (SEAL) programme and the theme 'Good to be me' could be used. This theme is about understanding feelings and how and why they lead us to behave in the way that we do; particularly being worried, anxious, surprised, disappointed, excited and proud.

Art: QCA Unit 4A – Viewpoints

Through this unit children explore how to convey the atmosphere and story of a dream. They invent a number of characters (monsters?) who are photographed on location and develop a narrative to describe the dream. They go on to make prints based on the narrative. This can link in a number of ways to the nightmare sequence of the dream. It can support Phase 2 of the narrative unit on creating a narrative using images of the settings.

Design and technology: QCA Unit 3C – Moving monsters

Through making a model of a monster that has moving parts controlled by pneumatics, the children develop an understanding of control through investigating simple pneumatic systems and designing a moving model.

Art and Design and Technology are blocked so children have more time during the week on that subject to enable continuity rather than spending time on just one lesson a week. The blocked work could be up to 4 hours a week to enable the recommended 8–12 hours for the QCA unit (Tables 8.1, 8.2, 8.3 and 8.4).

Games activities and non-fiction writing

This example will show how literacy and non-fiction instruction-writing learning outcomes can be delivered through games activities.

The games unit should be delivered or at least have progressed part way through, before the literacy non-fiction instruction-writing unit is started. The children should have progressed through the games unit so they are ready for QCA Games Unit Core Task 3.

The aim of this task is to make up a game using the skills, knowledge and understanding they have about the type of game activity they have been studying. Linking Core Task 3 with a non-fiction unit in literacy can support the children's understanding not only of games but of the instruction genre.

For children to write effective instructions for a game means they need to know how to play the game and understand it. The children need to work out how to communicate this game to their intended audience so they can play the game successfully. It may sound straightforward, but it actually takes considerable precision to design effective instructions.

It can be complicated to explain how to play a game if you have not done it yourself first. When writers work out instructions for recipes or craft activities, they usually create a rough plan, and then work through the process, amending and adding to their notes and diagrams as they go along. Once they have completed the process they then write it up carefully for their intended audience. In order for children to write clear instructions, they too usually need first-hand experience of the process concerned.

If children are encouraged to adopt a writer's approach, their ongoing notes or annotated plans of the games they design during PE Core Task 3 can be brought to the literacy hour to be developed into a finalised set of written instructions. Within the literacy sessions the teacher can ensure that pupils have also explored the language and structural features of a range of different instructional texts.

Example of using games and non-fiction writing

In a number of QCA games units, Core Task 3 asks the children to adapt the rules, equipment or skills of the game they are playing so that it suits them better. It also asks them to make up a game with a scoring system.

They should be able to play their game well and teach it to others in the class. This fits in perfectly with the non-fiction instruction unit in literacy. This task can use invasion, net/wall or striking and fielding type activities.

If children are to make up their own game and decide how to play it they will need to think about:

- rules;
- equipment;
- how to score;
- how to start and restart the game; and
- safety.

This can be linked with Core Task 3 from the games unit and either delivered during the literacy sessions, in allocated PE time, or a combination of the two. As the children devise their game they should be making notes and diagrams, and amending and annotating their notes as they go along.

During the literacy work the children will be studying examples of instructional texts, looking at design features, different layouts and the characteristics of instructional language, especially the use of imperative (bossy) verbs.

In shared writing one would demonstrate how to expand notes into instructional writing with the correct structure and characteristics.

The structure of an instruction text for games is often (but not always):

- goal – how to play a game;
- equipment listed in order, for example 6 cones, 1 skittle, 1 size-4 netball;
- sequenced steps to achieve the goal; and
- diagrams or illustrations.

The children then would expand their notes and diagrams into instructions that match the features of an instructional text. The set of instructions would be tested for effectiveness and then re-drafted if necessary before they are published, either written or through the use of ICT.

The above activity needs to be adapted to the requirements of the Key Stage 2 year group that it is aimed at. The following is a progression in writing instruction text using the 1998 Framework objectives:

Year 3, Term 2: T16, 17

Objective: Write instructions using a range of organisational devices (and using writing frames); make clear notes.

Year 4, Term 1: T25, 26

Objective: Write clear instructions, using link phrases and organisational conventions.

Year 5, Term 1: T25

Objective: To write instructional texts and test them out.
Shared work: Create a book of playground games for young children.

In the Primary Strategy (2006) the instructions unit is the second in a block of three non-fiction units in Year 3. It can be readily linked to other curriculum subjects and in this case it is PE and games. This is an example of linking – making games from PE Games Unit Core Task 3 and the instruction unit for Year 3 from the Primary Strategy.

Year 3 overview

- Read and follow instructions (e.g. a playground activity card).
- Give clear oral instructions to members of the group.
- Read and compare examples of instructional text, evaluating their effectiveness. Analyse more complicated instructions and identify organisational devices that make them easier to follow, for example lists, bullet points, numbered lists, diagrams with arrows, keys (e.g. playground activity card).
- Research designing a game (e.g. games core tasks from PE lessons) and work in small groups to prepare a set of instructions.
- Write clear instructions using correct register and devices to aid the reader. Evaluate effectiveness of instructions.

This non-fiction instruction unit from the Primary Strategy has three phases, with oral or written outcomes and assessment opportunities at regular intervals.

- Phase 1: reading and analysis of instructional texts.
- Phase 2: oral rehearsal; analysis; note-making and drafting.
- Phase 3: writing and evaluating instructional texts.

The 1998 Framework objectives covered by this unit and the three phases are:

- Year 3, Term 2: T12, T13, T14 and T15 – read and follow instructions; identify different purposes of instructional texts, evaluate usefulness and make comparisons; understand different ways to organise instructional texts.
- Year 3, Term 2: T16 – write instructions using a range of organisational devices and sequencing correctly.
- Year 3, Term 3: T24 – make alphabetically ordered texts. Use IT to bring to a published form.

Example using Year 3 Instruction Unit, Physical Education Games Unit and Core Task 3

Phase 1: reading and analysis of instructional texts

LEARNING OUTCOMES

- Children can recognise the structure and language features of an instructional text. This would be in preparation for the work on games but could use examples of playground activity cards or TOPS cards.

Phase 2: oral rehearsal; analysis; note-making and drafting

TEACHING CONTENT

- Decide on making a game, for example PE Core Task 3, or design a playground game for younger children.
- Children plan a logical sequence for the activity using knowledge gained from the games unit and orally rehearse and refine the detail of instructions. It is optional to record the activity with a digital video camera for reference.
- Using rehearsal session notes, for example video footage and diagrams, children draft the instructional sequence.
- Children research or create appropriate illustrations and graphics to support the instructional sequence.

LEARNING OUTCOME

Children can orally produce instructions, develop them into a chronological sequence and evaluate their effectiveness.

Phase 3: writing and evaluating instructional texts

TEACHING CONTENT

- Demonstrate how to write an instructional text using an example of notes of a game. Use the opportunity to demonstrate appropriate imperative simple sentence structure and punctuation.
- Children write their own instructional text following the same structure.
- Children read and follow instructional texts written by peers and play the game from the instructional texts. Discuss how effective the texts are to follow with reference to the use of appropriate language features.

LEARNING OUTCOME

Children can write an instructional text using selective adverbial language, sequenced imperative statements and presentational features such as bullet points or numbering.

This process can be adapted to fit in with other year groups within Key Stage 2 to meet the requirements of later non-fiction instruction units.

Gymnastic activities and ICT

This activity links the QCA ICT Unit 6A multimedia presentation and the integrated task with QCA Unit 6 gymnastic activities.

The aim of linking these units is to adapt the integrated task of the ICT unit so pupils can use the gymnastic sequences they create and use ICT to evaluate and improve the sequences over the sessions. The pupils would then have a multimedia record of their work from the early stages of their sequence to the finished product.

The focus throughout the gymnastic unit would be the QCA core task and how children evaluate and improve their sequence using ICT to develop their skills and sequences. The multimedia presentation will show how the children evaluated and improved their work until the final performance.

The audience for this presentation could be other children and parents or it could be used as a piece of work for transition into Key Stage 3. It could be put onto the school's website or used for assessment or even moderation among a number of schools in a school sport partnership. Both units would be delivered at the same time and prior learning for the ICT unit includes children having:

- experience of using a digital camera and importing the pictures to a PC; and
- experience of using a digital video camera and importing the video to a PC.

It is vital that children have these skills before using the equipment in the gymnastic sessions, otherwise the session can easily become an ICT session rather than one that uses ICT to enhance their gymnastics skills and sequence.

Prior learning for the gymnastic activities Unit 6 includes children having:

- performed a sequence of contracting actions;
- experienced matching and mirroring with a partner; and
- learned that ways of linking actions are as important as the actions themselves.

The aim of QCA gymnastic activities Unit 6 is that:

- The children will use their knowledge of compositional principles, for example how to use variations in speed, level and direction; how to combine and link actions; how to relate to partners and apparatus; and how to develop sequences that show an awareness of their audience.

The outcome for the gymnastic unit is that the children can perform the QCA core tasks.

Core task 1

Using what you know about a sequence create and perform for an audience a sequence on the floor and apparatus. It should include at least eight to ten elements. It must also include twisting and turning, flight, changes of direction and speed, and shapes and balances; for example, using small and large body parts.

Core task 2

Adapt the sequence created in Task 1 so that it can be performed in a small group of three or four people so that each person starts and finishes in a different place.

The learning objectives for Unit 6A are:

- to use a multimedia-authoring programme to organise, refine and present information in different forms for a specific audience; and

- to design pages and links that present the user with clear information.

Example of progression through both units

- ICT – Recap or teach how to use digital cameras and video cameras and input images into a suitable multimedia-authoring program.
    Task: children should work in small groups and take digital pictures and video of different types of balances. Input the pictures and video to a file.
- PE – Use the pictures and video to explore what makes a good balance. Ask children to evaluate their own and other members of their group's balances.
- ICT – Repeat ICT task of improved balances.

Within each gymnastic lesson the children should take pictures and/or video of their progress and save it to their file. As both units progress, the gymnastic work can be used within the ICT short focused tasks.

Unit 6A Section 1 – Setting the scene

LEARNING OUTCOMES

- Understand the potential of multimedia.

Unit 6A Section 2 – Short focused tasks

LEARNING OUTCOMES

- Recognise the features of good page design.

Children could create their front page using the balance pictures or video. They can start to think about the design of their presentation.

Unit 6A Section 3 – Short focused tasks

LEARNING OUTCOMES

- Create a page of sounds that are activated by named and correctly positioned buttons.

Children could add a picture or video that shows improvement and add a recording of the sound explaining what has improved and how they did it.

Unit 6A Section 4 – Short focused tasks

LEARNING OUTCOMES

- Organise sample screens and identify appropriate choiccs and links.

Children could produce a flowchart to identify links between pages and use action buttons.

Unit 6A Section 5 – Integrated task

LEARNING OUTCOMES

• Design multimedia pages with video, digital pictures and sound to present the audience with clear information about how your group evaluated and improved their sequence until the final performance.

Children use all the skills they have been taught to create their presentation of the finished core task.

Example of progression to gymnastic activity Core Task 1:

• Travelling, balancing, twisting and turning.
• Jumping and rolling, into and out of balances.
• Flight, into and out of balances.
• Counter balance with a partner.
• Revise counter balance, create a sequence of eight to ten elements.
• Perform and evaluate sequence with partner (Core Task 1).
• Perform pair sequence (with music if possible).

Throughout this progression the children will use cameras and video to evaluate their skills and sequence and put all the information into a file to use in their presentation. Within the gymnastic lessons the emphasis must be on the learning through the four strands and not on working out how to use ICT equipment.

The crossover between the two subjects will change, depending upon the knowledge and skills of the group of children, and you will need to adapt the process to meet their needs.

This could also be used as a theme for cross-curricular planning for Year 6. One example is shown in Figure 8.2.

Outdoor adventurous activities and science

Outdoor and adventurous activities can make a considerable contribution to pupils' learning in other National Curriculum areas. This example will explore how science learning outcomes can be met by using a digital photo trail.

Digital photo trails can be supervised by one class teacher and the whole class can take part in the activity. Digital photo trails develop similar skills to orienteering, but in this activity a science task for the children to complete before moving on to the next part of the trail is placed at each control card.

This digital photo trail activity could link with the theme of habitats (QCA Science Unit 4B – Habitats).

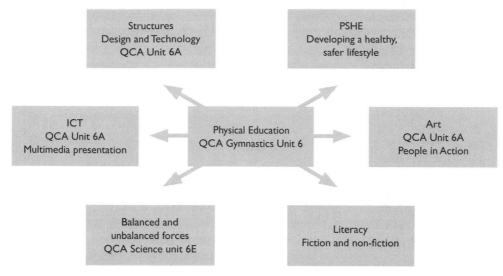

Figure 8.2 Gymnastics: QCA Unit 6 links.

Learning objective

* Group organisms according to observable features.

Learning outcome

* To understand how animals can be grouped according to criteria.

This activity could also link with the QCA ICT unit 'Branching databases' to further link the work on keys and branching databases.

In this example mini-beasts have been used, and at each control the children group mini-beasts in one of two ways:

* The children will use a classification key to group the mini-beasts (Figure 8.3).
* The children will record the observable features of the mini-beasts onto their control card then devise their own key to group the mini-beasts later back in the classroom.

Classification keys are an invaluable identification tool and the essence of a good key is to identify something that asks a series of yes/no questions. A simple key is a good starting point for children to classify materials or, in this case, mini-beasts. The first question of a key should split the material or object into sets of two. The first question used on this key was to ask: 'Woodland mini-beasts, legs or no legs?' Then, if the answer was 'no legs', the next question on the flowchart was 'shell or no shell?' (see Figure 8.3 for the key).

The digital photo trail does need to be carefully organised and properly prepared (Figure 8.4).

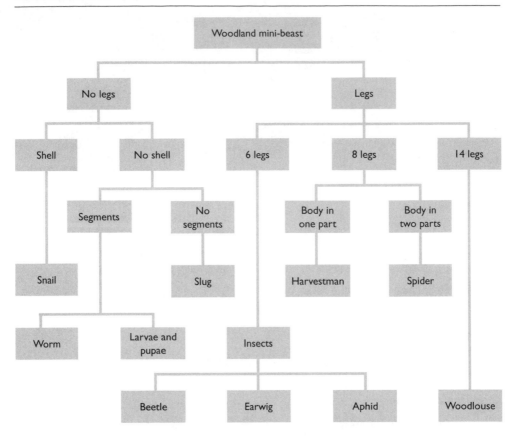

Figure 8.3 Woodland mini-beasts flowchart.

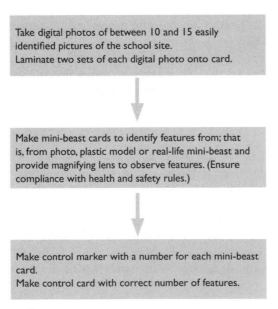

Figure 8.4 Digital photo trail.

Digital photo trail activity

The children work in pairs or small groups and are given or take a digital photo out of a box with a number on it. This digital photo is of a feature on the school site. (This could be the whole site or a section of the site. Ensure the children understand the boundaries and the areas out of bounds, for example where vehicles may be moving.)

The children travel to the place on the digital photo and find the control marker with the mini-beast card. The children use their key to identify the mini-beast and record what the mini-beast is on their control card against the number that matches up with the number on their digital photo (Figure 8.5).

The children return their digital photo and are given or take a new one and then travel to the next control marker and identify the mini-beast and record it using the control card. This continues until the children's control card is completed (Table 8.6).

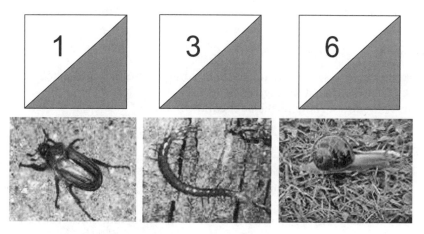

Figure 8.5 Example of mini-beast control markers.

Table 8.6 Control card

Control number	Mini-beast
1	
2	
3	
4	
5	
6	
7	
8	
9	
10	
11	
12	

An adaptation to this activity could be a continuous digital photo trail:

- Children are given a different digital photo of where to start from.
- Children travel to their start place and find the control marker with the mini-beast card and carry out the task of recording the features.
- So that children do not need to return to the start the control marker will also have a digital photo of another part of the school site, which shows where they will find the next control marker.
- Children travel to the next control marker and continue to follow the digital photos until they find the marker that shows their starting control marker. The children travel back to the start.

The main outcome of the lesson, which is a science lesson, would be to ensure that the children can group animals and explain criteria on which the groups are based. This activity can also support outdoor and adventurous activities skills such as:

Acquiring and developing skills

- Look at the photos carefully to ensure children run to the right place.
- Look carefully when deciding which way to go.
- Choose the fastest route to the next control.

Selecting and applying skills

- Understand the task and know how to approach it.
- Record or collect the information carefully and accurately at the control sites.

This activity can easily be adapted to meet the learning outcomes from a variety of curriculum subjects.

Athletics activities in mathematics and ICT

There are many opportunities for athletics to be taught across the curriculum, but this example will look strictly at mathematics and ICT.

Performances can be recorded and by using ICT, databases can be set up to record data and track children's performances at the end of the unit and also over the Key Stage to check for progress. However, this is only a record of performance – for assessment in National Curriculum PE, a child should be assessed against the four strands of learning: acquiring and developing skills; selecting and applying skills; evaluating performance; and knowledge and understanding of fitness and health.

Measuring is one of the seven core learning outcomes in the Primary Framework for mathematics. These outcomes are organised into five blocks. The two blocks that could be used with athletic activities are Block C, 'Handling data and measures', and Block D, 'Calculating, measuring and understanding shape'.

One mathematics objective that can be delivered through athletic activities is knowing the relationship between kilometres and metres, and metres and centimetres; and choosing and using appropriate units to estimate, measure and record measurements. The recording of these measurements could then be added to a database.

A mathematics lesson could use athletic activities to meet the objective above. The children could estimate how far they can throw various objects, for example beanbags and shuttlecocks. They throw the object and then measure the distance thrown and record it. A carousel of activities could be set up, for example throwing, jumping and running. The children have to estimate how far they can throw or jump, or how long they can run in a certain time. They then perform the activity and measure and record the results.

However, the learning outcome of the lesson is related to the children's mathematical understanding of estimating and measuring and not on their technique. (The athletics lessons as part of their PE curriculum should be used to work on their technique.)

When planned in advance, the mathematics lesson could be used as the baseline for children's attainment in athletics. By recording an initial score and then repeating the mathematics lesson at the end of the unit, the children's progress in performance and in estimating and measuring can be compared.

The Norwich Union Shine Awards and Elevating Athletics are resources that can support athletics across the curriculum, and the Youth Sport Trust resource 'Get Moving, Get Learning' also has examples of using athletic activities with mathematics.

Bibliography

BAALPE, CCPR, PEAUK (2005) *Declaration from the National Summit on Physical Education*. London: British Association of Advisors and Lecturers in Physical Education, CCPR, Physical Education Association of the United Kingdom.

DfEE (1998) *National Literacy Strategy: Framework for Teaching*. London: Department for Education and Employment.

DfES (2001) *National Literacy Strategy: Framework for Teaching*. London: Department for Education and Skills.

DfES (2003) *Excellence and Enjoyment*. London: Department for Education and Skills.

DfES (2006) *Primary Framework for Literacy and Mathematics*. London: Department for Education and Skills.

DfES (2007) *Primary National Strategy*. London: Department for Education and Skills.

Outdoor Education Advisers Panel (2005) TOP Outdoors, Youth Sport Trust.

QCA (2007) *Schemes of Work*. London: Qualifications and Curriculum Authority.

Chapter 9

Creativity matters

Patrick Smith

The tragic death of Victoria Climbié in 2000 and the subsequent report by Lord Laming (2003) led to the introduction of the Children Act (DfES 2004). As a result, the Act necessitated a cooperative approach to integrate services across former education authorities, children's social services, local learning and skills councils, police authorities and primary care trusts. It is expected that all authorities will have such integrated services in place by 2008.

Following the Act the Green Paper *Every Child Matters* (ECM) (DfES 2003) was introduced, driven by the need to share information across sectors, primarily for the protection and well-being of children, as mentioned in the Bichard Inquiry in 2004. However, government ministers decided that such a remit was not encompassing enough as it did not necessarily take into consideration older children, 13–19 year olds and, consequently, the Green Paper *Youth Matters* was published in July 2005 and *Youth Matters: Next Steps* in 2006. The *Youth Matters* paper tasked authorities, among other things, to develop new and innovative ways of delivering services to young people to bring real and positive changes to their lives.

These proposals provide tangible opportunities for schools, teachers and the PE fraternity to make such positive changes happen so that we do transform children's lives. Here is an opportunity for us to be creative and to reflect on our philosophy for PE, our curriculum (perhaps tired and traditional), our pedagogy (is it varied and inspirational?) and the whole child's PE experience in our schools. And does our curriculum prepare and encourage a high percentage of children to partake in physical activity once they have left school?

The five outcomes of the *Every Child Matters* agenda are:

1 Be healthy: enjoying good physical and mental health and living a healthy lifestyle.
2 Be safe: being protected from harm and abuse.
3 Enjoy and achieve: getting the most out of life and developing the skills needed for adulthood.
4 Make a positive contribution: being involved with the community and society and not engaging in anti-social or offending behaviour.
5 Achieve economic well-being: not being prevented by economic disadvantage from achieving their full potential in life.

This proposal has without doubt marked a major watershed in the history of how services operate (integrated) and, more specifically, has and will have a major impact on young people's welfare, but the concept is not necessarily new to the PE fraternity:

> The past twenty-five or thirty years have been marked by the progressive recognition of the State in securing the physical well-being of children and young persons.
>
> (Board of Education 1933: 6)

This suggests that such needs of children and young people were well recognised from the early 1900s. It just took 100 years to implement.

The contribution that PE can make to the ECM agenda is one that can have a significant impact on children's well-being. It is so encouraging to see the first outcome of 'be healthy: enjoying good physical and mental health and living a healthy lifestyle'. Let me dwell on this for a moment. No other subject can make such an impact as PE. In fact, it would not be too presumptuous to state that our subject can be the driving force behind the delivery of the ECM agenda, but we must seize the opportunity to do so and get it right.

What does the first outcome mean and how can we enable it? If we intend our children to be healthy does it really mean that we need to send our Year 9 girls on a cross-country run in the pouring rain in January while the gym is being used for exams? And while we are about it, will we have them running in gym knickers and short skirts too? Why do we insist on testing all our Year 7 pupils on the Bleep Test as an excuse to measure fitness and to produce statistical analysis of their performances as a further misguided venture into the use of ICT in PE? My children and yours have probably experienced both. However, there is some excellent practice out there in our schools, delivered by brilliant teachers, and it is a shame that such practices are not celebrated widely enough.

To teach children how to stay safe can also be part of their PE programme and implicit within the curricular areas of PE, but the wider implications are perhaps more significant in that through positive physical experiences children will want to be physically active after school hours and indeed once they have finished full-time education. Consequently, we would hope this would contribute to a reduction in, for example, drug abuse, petty crime and more serious criminal offences. Consider for one moment how many young people continue to throw a javelin, shot or discus once they have left school. Such activities may be well placed to teach safety but are not necessarily justifiable in their current form where they dominate a PE curriculum's summer programme for up to 4 or 5 years.

For children to *enjoy and achieve* and for them to make the most out of life so that they develop their skills for adulthood, we must become much more aware of our children's needs. We should not just cater for the very able child, or for that matter the less able, but for all. This indeed is a real challenge when teaching large groups of children but PE teachers have proved that they know the children in their care very well and can be a real asset in determining pastoral care solutions. Central to children's needs, and particularly in PE lessons, is self-esteem. Girls often struggle with body image and boys who are less able in the traditional sports sometimes feel isolated from their more able peers. Throw into the equation the irregular pattern of children's growth and development (Cale and Harris 2004) and it becomes almost impossible for many children to enjoy and achieve.

To be creative in PE does not necessarily mean throwing the baby out with the bathwater. The contributors to this book firmly acknowledge the place of competition within the PE curriculum. We also acknowledge the value of teaching the traditional games and activities such as soccer, hockey, rugby and netball. Indeed, many of us played such sports at representative level. What we are asking physical educators to do is to be creative within their teaching of these traditional sports and to acknowledge the value not only of doing things differently but teaching and learning different activities too that may engage children more readily. Consequently, it is not necessarily *what* you teach but *how* you teach it.

The traditional sports and activities will, for some pupils, enable them to make a positive contribution by involving them in clubs after school while they play with and coach other young people. However, a non-traditional approach to PE through the introduction of alternative activities (which many schools do), such as self-defence, street dance, Ultimate Frisbee, Aussie rules, handball, water polo and so on, may well not only engage pupils more in their learning but, perhaps more importantly, engage them in lifelong physical activity.

Economic well-being – if interpreted along the lines of being free from such disadvantages that inhibit children from achieving their full potential in life – is a difficult nut to crack. We can only do our best as teachers by providing children with the best possible start in life by giving them a breadth of opportunities. From such opportunities children may well find something they excel at or enjoy for enjoyment's sake. Without some breadth to the curriculum children may never find their true potential. It is often interesting hearing children talk about how they play off a handicap of eight (golf) or that they are regional champion at sailing or a black belt in judo, yet they were rarely introduced to such sports at school but somehow (perhaps through parental support) found their way. Can we not help others to find their way too, and could this be by providing further opportunities through the curriculum?

> Physical education helps pupils become physically skilful, competent young people who make physical activity a central part of their lives, both in and out of school.
> (QCA 2006)

The curriculum aims as outlined by the Qualifications and Curriculum Authority (QCA) are ones that are not difficult to sign up to:

- successful learners – who progress and achieve;
- confident individuals – who lead safe and healthy lives; and
- responsible citizens – who make a positive contribution to society, given that they are drawn directly from the ECM agenda.

The QCA also suggest that a wide range of skills and activities should be provided so that children do discover their own aptitudes and preferences at school that lead them towards lifelong physical activity.

The key concept of competences in physical activity which comprise physical skills, application of skills, and capacity of body and mind could therefore be delivered through a varied menu of physical activities with, when appropriate, a performance focus. The key processes can also be delivered creatively as children develop a variety of techniques, achieve success, develop their physical strength and mental determination and evaluate their strengths and areas for development.

The range and content of the proposed new curriculum, which includes *outwitting opponents*, can be delivered through many mediums and not just those outlined by the QCA (although they do mention Gaelic football, American football, fencing, judo and karate, which is commendable) but could also include outwitting opponents in outdoor and adventurous activities, for example in sailing or kayaking races where tactics and strategies are vital to effective performance.

The *accurate replication* of actions can also be learnt through many different physical activities and we note the inclusion of dance and gymnastics and welcome the inclusion of skateboarding as an alternative medium too. To combine gymnastics, dance, trampolining and rebound tumbling reminds me of a recent live performance of the Cirque du Soleil; such a performance would serve as real inspiration for many of our children, truly athletes at their very best. Indeed, France still has a limited number of high-performance circus schools that train children and young people in the arts of tightrope walking, juggling and associated skills.

Exploring and communicating involves children measuring their own and others' performances through competition against themselves and others and QCA suggest that this can be realised through a variety of activities, so how about archery and golf? *Identifying and solving problems* could be achieved through, for example, outdoor and adventurous activities, though we should not necessarily assume that problem-solving in itself is sufficient, rather that we enable the children to take some responsibility for setting the problems too rather than being just the passive recipients of the task.

Exercising safely and effectively may be built around many different activities too. Perhaps this is an area that may need some further investigation and review, in terms of current practice. The notion of risk is one that is welcomed (Mortlock 2000) but risk assessment must be sufficiently carried out whether the children are working outdoors or off-site, or following an exercise programme in a fitness room or gymnasium. However, if we can provide children with appropriate activities and surroundings that perhaps emulate those they will find in adult life, we will be well on the way to preparing them for lifelong physical activity.

Part of our creativity in the PE curriculum should be driven by the diverse nature of the children in our care. We know from national statistics that the percentage of children who have a language other than English as their first language has risen rapidly over the last decade (1997–2007). Indeed, over 50 per cent of children in inner London-maintained primary schools now have English as an additional language and the figure is not much lower for our maintained secondary schools, at about 46 per cent. Although the picture across the country is not so high it is not insignificant, with schools in the West Midlands showing a high proportion of children whose first language is known or believed to be other than English. Consequently, with a very high proportion of children that come from different cultures attending schools, we should be making a positive effort to evolve our curriculum from essentially white middle-class games – gymnastics, swimming and athletics – to one that is far more inclusive. Here lies, perhaps, a major need for staff development but I am sure such moves would raise participation levels among children who come from such varied social, cultural and religious backgrounds.

The possibilities of making a real impact on the behaviour of children and raising the levels of attainment of pupils as well as their self-esteem is one that should also be explored through a creative approach to teaching and learning in PE. Her Majesty's Chief Inspector for Schools (HMCI) made it quite clear in his annual report for 2004/2005 (Ofsted 2005) that behaviour is only satisfactory in many of our secondary schools and that pupil disruption has a significant impact on the quality of teaching and learning.

The Steer Report (2005), which focused on behaviour in schools, was explicit in identifying that the quality of teaching and learning and the behaviour of pupils are inseparable issues and are the responsibilities of all staff. The Report does not identify a single solution to the problem but does recognise that through good practice in teaching and learning, effective behaviour management, strong school leadership and liaison with parents and carers such problems are manageable.

Many schools are already offering very different activities for their 'difficult children', which is commendable, but care should be taken with this approach which may well breed contempt from those more placid pupils who too would like to go bowling but are confined to the classroom or soccer field during the winter months. Let us reward the well-behaved children too by providing them with a challenging and innovative curriculum.

The Professional Standards for Teachers (TDA 2007) form part of a wider framework of standards for the whole school workforce. The framework provides professional standards for:

- the award of qualified teacher status (QTS) (Q);
- teachers on the main scale (Core) (C);
- teachers on the upper pay scale (Post Threshold Teachers) (P);
- excellent Teachers (E); and
- advanced skills teachers (ASTs) (A).

This framework has three interrelated sections that cover:

- professional attributes;
- professional knowledge and understanding; and
- professional skills.

Underpinning these new standards for classroom teachers are the five key outcomes for children and young people identified in ECM. Now we have some joined-up thinking so that ECM permeates the new standards and the revised curriculum at Key Stage 3.

It is not the purpose of this chapter to discuss the merits of these standards or indeed critique them; however, it will be useful to make a brief analysis of how these standards may enable teachers to be more creative in the work that they do.

Central to the new standards is identifying and supporting the professional development needs of teachers so that they are sustained, relevant and effective. That teachers are up to date in terms of subject knowledge and pedagogy is also clearly identified.

It should not, however, be the sole responsibility of ASTs to provide models of excellent and innovative teaching but all teachers should be seeking to be innovative and creative too. It is clear that such practices of excellent and innovative delivery will impact positively on pupils' learning and consequently contribute to whole-school improvement. It is pertinent to point out too that as part of teachers' personal and professional development, standard Q8 is most relevant and that teachers should:

> Have a creative and constructively critical approach towards innovation, being prepared to adapt their practice where benefits and improvements are identified.
> (Training and Development Agency 2007: 8)

The Office for Standards in Education (Ofsted) in *Expect the Unexpected* (2003) have sought to encourage creativity and innovation in both primary and secondary schools. This makes a refreshing change given the government's obsession (and as a consequence that of schools) with results and league tables. Somehow, we have managed to lose sight of what really matters as we teach to the exams and pupils are treated as empty vessels, mechanistically shunted toward the examination checkout. I hope that the ECM agenda and the new curriculum proposals will deliver the flexibility and creativity that pupils deserve.

As someone who has taught and inspected PE in schools for a number of years I have witnessed some excellent teaching and creative and innovative practices. I remember inspecting a school in the north of England where the dance teacher (a member of an external dance organisation) arrived full of enthusiasm. She had a bright purple top to match her bright purple hair and she taught the best session of street dance with a group of Year 10 girls that I have ever seen. There were no non-participants, the girls were fully engaged in their learning, the lesson was pacey and progression was rapid. My only wish at the time was that my own daughter could be there to join in. An Ofsted inspector with a tear in his eye: that is something you do not expect to see very often.

Another inspection I did in the north-east of England was in a large mixed comprehensive school. The PE department comprised a really strong team of committed teachers and the relationships with the pupils were strong, and as such behaviour was generally very good. I witnessed a Year 9 boys' hockey lesson in which the teacher taught a well-structured warm-up followed by a lengthy but quite purposeful skills development phase and finally a short applied games phase followed by a cool-down. It was a cold day, the pupils were well motivated and they were desperate to play the game at the end of the session. It was a very good lesson but I felt that there was a missed opportunity here whereby the teacher could have tried something different, for example started with the game after the warm-up and extracted one or two skills from the game to work on. When I asked the teacher at the end of the lesson why he structured the session in the way that he did, his reply was 'that's what I expected you wanted to see'. I was really disappointed. My view is that Ofsted and its inspectors must encourage and support innovative and creative methods of teaching and learning by reporting on it and making it clear to the profession that when appropriate it can be a real asset in supporting pupils' learning.

Girls and boys street dancing, following classes in self-defence, working on the dry ski-slope to record and analyse technique, playing handball, working with ICT packages to analyse their own and others' performances in cricket, coaches working effectively with pupils and teachers, pupils devising their own fitness programmes and working on them in their fitness suite, student teachers supporting pupils in school outside the confines of teaching practice, really engaging pupils with restricted mobility (from cerebral palsy), Muslim girls fully involved in their learning in athletics: these are just some of the things I have witnessed in my visits to schools. There are many brilliant teachers of PE out there who really are creating a future for our children so that they do indeed involve themselves in lifelong physical activity.

Bibliography

Bichard, M. (2004) *The Bichard Inquiry Report, House of Commons*. London: The Stationery Office.

Board of Education (1933) *Syllabus of Physical Training for Schools*. London: His Majesty's Stationery Office.

Cale, L. and Harris J. (2004) *Exercise and Young People: Issues, Implications and Initiatives*. Basingstoke: Palgrave and Macmillan.

DfES (2003) *Every Child Matters, Green Paper presented to Parliament by the Chief Secretary to The Treasury*. London: Department for Education and Skills.

DfES (2004) *The Children Act*. London: The Stationery Office.

DfES (2005) *Youth Matters, Green Paper*. London: House of Commons.

DfES (2006) *Youth Matters: Next Steps*. London: Department for Education and Skills Publications.

Laming, W. H. (2003) *The Victoria Climbié Enquiry*. London: Westminster.

Mortlock, C. (2000) *The Adventure Alternative*. Milnthorpe, Cumbria: Cicerone Press.

Ofsted (2003) *Expect the Unexpected: Promoting Creativity in Education*. London: Ofsted Publications.

Ofsted (2005) *HMCI Report 2004/2005*. London: The Stationery Office.

QCA (2006) *Programmes of Study: Physical Education*. London: Qualifications and Curriculum Authority.

Smith, P. (1998) 'The French Experience', *Bulletin of Physical Education*, 34(3): 212–217.

Steer, A. (2005) *Learning Behaviour: The Report of the Practitioner Group on School Behaviour and Discipline*. Available online at www.teachernet.gov.uk/publications.

TDA (2007) *Professional Standards for Teachers*. Training and Development Agency Publications.

Index